To WD and PG

THE UNIVERSITY OF
WINCHESTER

brilliant

Graduate
Career
Handbook

Judith Done and Rachel Mulvey

Prentice Hall
is an imprint of

PEARSON

Harlow, England • London • New York • Boston • San Francisco • Toronto • Sydney • Singapore • Hong Kong
Tokyo • Seoul • Taipei • New Delhi • Cape Town • Madrid • Mexico City • Amsterdam • Munich • Paris • Milan

Pearson Education Limited
Edinburgh Gate
Harlow
Essex CM20 2JE
England

and Associated Companies throughout the world

Visit us on the World Wide Web at:
www.pearsoned.co.uk

First published 2011

ISBN: 978-0-273-74488-7

British Library Cataloguing-in-Publication Data
A catalogue record for this book is available from the British Library

10 9 8 7 6 5 4 3 2 1
15 14 13 12 11

Typeset in 10/14 Plantin by 30
Printed and bound in Great Britain by Ashford Colour Press Ltd, Gosport

About the authors

Dr Judith Done is a visiting fellow at the University of Chester, where she was, until recently, Director of Careers and Employability. She is a fellow of the Institute of Career Guidance (ICG) and an associate fellow of the British Psychological Society.

Her working life has been spent in career guidance as a practitioner, trainer and manager. Her research interests are in career guidance, personal development and interpersonal communication.

Judith is a volunteer advice worker, school governor and occasional freelance trainer.

Professor Rachel Mulvey holds a chair in career guidance at the University of East London, where she is Associate Dean of Psychology. She has recently developed an online game to help undergraduates develop their employability.

For many years, Rachel worked as a careers adviser in schools and colleges, also broadcasting on the subject on Radio 1 and Radio 4. Her latest research is a pan-European project on innovation in the training of career guidance professionals.

Rachel is a former president of the Institute of Career Guidance.

Contents

Acknowledgements

We are very grateful to colleagues and friends in career guidance and higher education for the many and varied contributions they have made to the development of this handbook, and to our families for their unwavering encouragement and support. We would like to acknowledge the generosity of all the people we refer to in our brilliant examples, and quote in our brilliant quotes. Our thanks also to the warden and staff of Gladstone's Library, who have no idea how helpful they were in providing the perfect writers' retreat at a critical stage.

Particular thanks are due to Helen Webster of the University of Chester for her practical help, and to Jane Artess for permission for us to draw freely on the Higher Education Careers Services Unit (HECSU) publication *What do graduates do?* Finally, our heartfelt thanks to Steve Temblett, our commissioning editor, for his reassurance, expertise and enthusiasm.

Introduction

Notes for tutors

How this book can work for you

We were able to write this book because career guidance is our specialism. Between us we have a span of experience including practice, management, practitioner training, research and broadcasting. We feel confident we know what we're talking about, and we think we can help students to manage their career well. We also believe we can help fellow tutors.

The accidental tutor

We understand that being asked to deliver on careers or employability when your own area of expertise is *The 19th Century Epistolary Novel*, *Conflict Resolution in Contested States*, or *Lung Function in Elite Athletes*, can trigger a wide range of perfectly reasonable responses: from irritation through frustration to fear. This book can help you out because it has everything you need in one place. So, if you are a personal tutor, the employability coordinator in your department, or you simply want to be able to respond when students come to you for help and advice, this book is for you.

The specialist tutor

If you yourself are a specialist, perhaps leading or teaching on an assessed module (in careers and employability or career management skills), this book will work for you and for your students. Unlike other careers handbooks, we explain how the graduate labour market operates, and have used a lot of labour market information. This is in addition to the practical know-how about career planning and job applications that all students need at some stage, and many students told us they wanted. Although written for students and graduates, there are exercises and tasks that you could build in to taught sessions and workshops. For example, Chapter 2 'The graduate labour market' and Chapter 3 'Labour market information: analysis of what graduates do' both offer a theoretical and knowledge base for your teaching on skills and employability modules. You could also use Chapter 9 'Dates and deadlines: your timeline for action' and Chapter 10 'Making applications: getting past the first post' to structure your tutorial input. We hope you find this book works alongside your input, and enhances both the teaching and learning experience.

Notes for careers advisers

Extensive use of labour market information

This book differs from other career handbooks aimed at students and graduates in the extent to which we have included labour market information (LMI), and have given clear advice to readers on how to access and make use of LMI. We recognise that you know your students and their courses and the employment patterns of your graduates, and you know your local and regional labour market. We hope that this handbook, with its broader LMI perspective, will be a useful addition to your practice and a helpful reference for your students.

Working with academic colleagues to share expertise

Strong partnerships with academic colleagues, based on mutual understanding, lead to provision for students which builds on careers advisers' expertise and tutors' specialist subject knowledge. Please have a look at our 'Notes for tutors' for our thoughts about how this handbook might support your academic colleagues – and indeed you yourselves – in the planning and delivery of workshops, seminars and taught modules.

We hope to enhance your existing offer to students

We hope you will find that this handbook enhances the work you do with students and graduates – it certainly isn't designed to replace it. You will see that we frequently signpost students and graduates to their university careers service. We hope that you will welcome this. While we know that there are differences in style, provision and resources in different universities, we hope you will be able to respond if readers come your way.

Notes for Parents Plus

We know that behind every successful graduate, there are people rooting for them, willing them on, wanting them to achieve their potential. We use the term parents plus to include anyone who is 'behind' a graduate. If you are one of those people (you may be a grandparent, friend, or partner) whatever your relationship, this is a good book for you – and for your graduate. (Of course, we think it would make a brilliant present!)

Look beyond the headlines on graduate employment

You might be concerned about your graduate: you might think they should be doing something about getting a job, even though all their time is taken up with the course and perhaps some paid work. You might even be wondering what was the point of them working so hard for their degree, given the gloomy headlines about graduate jobs. However, if you look beyond the headlines, you will find that there are jobs, although securing a brilliant job might take time and effort. This book shows your graduate how to navigate the graduate labour market, and how to keep going when it gets tough.

The 21st-century graduate faces a different job market

We also have a message for you, which is this. If you are basing your advice on your own experience of getting your first job, *particularly* if you are a graduate, your advice is out of date. The graduate labour market has changed: there are fewer jobs and employers now expect graduates to develop their skills before they start work. To do this, your graduate might have to take on unpaid work, take up an internship, take a fixed-term contract or start with a non-graduate job. None of these reflects badly on your graduate: this is simply how the graduate labour market works in the 21st century.

Keep an open mind and challenge your graduate to do so too

In this book, we support your graduate, but we also challenge them. We go so far as to tell them that any job is better than no job, and that even the most lowly task can help them build up the know-how they need as they work. We know you are behind your graduate, so don't despair: keep an open mind, and support them as they carve out their own path towards their brilliant career.

Notes on our brilliant examples and brilliant quotes

Brilliant examples

In this book you will see brilliant examples in most chapters. These quotes are by real students and graduates, drawn from a range of universities and subject disciplines. We also approached people working in small to medium-sized enterprises (SMEs) because that is an important employment sector. All were kind enough to let us quote their stories and we have used their own words, with their permission. We are very grateful to them for their willingness to share their experiences in this book. We've chosen these brilliant examples because they bring to life some of the key messages in this handbook. We also hope that these brilliant examples will inspire and encourage you.

Brilliant quotes

We know that whatever we say, as career guidance professionals, it's good too for you to hear direct from employers. So we approached two people, with different perspectives, and asked them to tell us what key messages they want graduates to hear. We are very grateful to both of them for their willingness to be included in this way. You'll see them quoted in most of the chapters in the book, so let us introduce them to you.

Carl Gilleard is the Chief Executive of the Association of Graduate Recruiters (AGR). AGR is dedicated to supporting and representing employers in all aspects of graduate recruitment and development. It represents over 800 organisations that, between them, offer a high proportion of graduate opportunities in the UK.

Julian Radley is Financial Director of Evotel Holdings, which supplies televisions to electrical retailers, and operates across the UK, Europe and the Far East. Nearly 60 per cent of private sector employment in the UK is located in small to medium-sized enterprises. Evotel, his highly successful company, is a brilliant example of the kind of SME that is vital to the economy.

How to use this handbook

If you are an undergraduate or recent graduate, this handbook is for you. We hope that you will use it frequently, dipping in to whichever topics are relevant to you at the time. Like other careers handbooks we will give you pointers for applying for jobs. However, unlike other careers handbooks, we will help you to understand the graduate labour market, as we believe that this is fundamental to planning for and achieving your brilliant graduate career. Throughout the book we illustrate and reinforce our key messages with brilliant features – tips, dos and don'ts, quotes, case studies and recaps – and we hope you find them useful.

What do you hope to do after university?

The obvious answer to this question is: to get a job that recognises your talents, offers you the chance to shine, allows you to do interesting things and ideally to earn enough money to have a good lifestyle and to pay back your student loan. You could call that the *Brilliant Graduate Career* answer.

However, in the real world, the answer could be very different. Your first step might be to get a job, any job, just to pay the bills. This may be a service sector job in a supermarket, bar or fast-food outlet, perhaps a job you did part-time while at university – which might make you wonder why you bothered to go to university in the first place. If that's where you are at the moment, or where you think you might be in the future, read on. We'll help you to see how any job can help you, even in a small way, work towards your brilliant career. The key is is to be positive and assume that there will be a good outcome eventually – though perhaps not straight away.

Your options

Your first step after graduation is usually one of the following choices:

- A graduate entry job: by this we mean a job that demands a degree, and we include graduate training schemes.

- A direct entry job: you don't need a degree for the job but having a degree will speed your progression and may help with promotion, e.g. police or retail management. A direct entry job can be a key step in your career plan; it can be your active choice.

- A direct entry job by default: likely to be your fall-back plan, perhaps because of a shortage of graduate opportunities. You can definitely use this for extending your professional repertoire to gain leverage in the graduate job market.

- Time out by choice, e.g. for travel, perhaps to work abroad, or just for taking stock.

- Postgraduate study: either to qualify for a particular job or for love of the subject (vocational/professional or academic).

- Self-employment – starting your own business.

More than one option

Of course, you could follow more than one of these options in sequence. For example, you could have a year of working abroad then take up post-graduate study or get a job. Or you might need a year of postgraduate, vocational study before you can enter a graduate-entry job like teaching or law. Taking a longer view, you might decide, some years after leaving university, that you are ready to take on more study, either part-time or full-time.

One handbook, in two halves

What's out there, or part one

Deciding what to do after university is very personal; not just what you decide, but when you decide, is different for everyone. Even if you have come to university with a very clear career choice in mind, you may choose, in the light of experience, to change your career plan, or even to change your university course; and, even if you yourself don't waver from your original career thinking, the graduate labour market may have changed around you. So, in the first part of this book we will help you to get to know and understand the graduate labour market so that you will be well prepared. We will set out the popular options for graduates – travel and how to get the most from it, postgraduate study, and graduate training schemes – and flag up those where forward planning is needed. Finding out more about your options is a good first step – it doesn't commit you but it starts to equip you. We will help you to avoid putting your head in your hands and wailing: 'If only I'd known sooner – why did nobody tell me?'.

How to make the most of what's out there, or part two

In the second part of this handbook we will focus on what you can do to influence your graduate career. Unlimited choice sounds great in theory, but in practice it can be overwhelming. If someone offers you the chance to travel to anywhere in the world, that can be a surprisingly difficult choice, and the prospect of what to do after university might feel a bit like that. A good career plan involves a narrowing down of options under serious consideration as you progress through university – but with some flexibility built in for when setbacks occur. We will help you first with some strategies for making connections between what's out there and you as an individual, with your unique package of strengths, interests and circumstances. Then we will give you some good tips and tactics for getting into the labour market, in particular, how to seek out and make the most of experiences and opportunities. We believe that, regardless of the state of the job market, a positive, proactive approach is vital; and we hope that this book will help you to adopt our view.

PART 1

What's out there

CHAPTER 1

Accessing job opportunities

Headlines will always be negative: look beyond them. The market is tough – but there are always vacancies.

Carl Gilleard, Chief Executive, Association of Graduate Recruiters

This chapter looks at how employers get their vacancies into the market-place, which means we show you where the job opportunities are, and how you can find them. It is important to remember that employers are looking for the right person to fill their job with just as much commitment and concern as you show when you are looking for your brilliant job.

Supply and demand: it takes two

The basic principle of the graduate labour market is that two equally important elements must be in place for the market to work, namely: supply and demand (for an in-depth exploration of the graduate labour market, have a look at Chapter 2). In the graduate labour market you as the jobseeker are the supply, and the employer offering the job is the demand. Clearly, for the job market to function at all, both supply and demand each need to know of the other's existence, which means that you (supply) have to make your presence in the marketplace known, and the employers (demand) equally have to make it known that they have a job that they want to fill.

 **definitions**

> You, the jobseeker, are the **supply side** of the graduate labour market; the employers are the **demand side**.

The employer's perspective

For an employer, taking on a new person is a big deal. It is going to increase their payroll, it is probably going to cost them money just to get their vacancy publicised and, when they do find someone, they are going to have to allocate time (which is a valuable resource) to integrate the new employee into the workplace quickly, so that they can function well and be a valued addition to the organisation. Employers care a great deal about getting the right person for the job. They don't want a huge range of applicants: what they want is to choose from a range of suitable candidates so that they recruit the right one for their job, which is why employers are keen to get their job out there where people can see it. They can use a range of media to do this: print, online and networking (sometimes called word of mouth). Instead of responding to job vacancies that are advertised, you can take the initiative and approach an employer to see if there is a possible vacancy; this is called a speculative application. You can also choose to work for yourself, rather than work for someone else, namely self-employment. So let's look at each of these in turn.

How employers get their jobs out there

Vacancies in print

Newspapers

Print media comprises newspapers, magazines and directories. In some cases, the vacancies advertised will only be a small part of the publication. This is the case with newspapers, for example. The national newspapers (including *The Times*, the *Daily Telegraph*, the *Guardian* and the *Independent*) often group vacancies by sector and publish all those vacancies on the same day each week, e.g. education jobs appear in the *Guardian* on Tuesdays. You need to check with the individual newspaper title to see what cluster of job adverts are published on which day of the week. Newspapers also publish supplements given over exclusively to job vacancies. This can be by sector (engineering or social care) or by level (graduate jobs). As these supplements tend to be occasional rather than regular you'll need to keep an eye out for announcements which appear in the paper itself.

brilliant tip

Check the national quality newspapers to see what kind of job vacancies are advertised on which day of the week.

Regional and local papers

You have plenty of choice when it comes to local and regional papers: over 1,500 titles are listed in the UK. Some publish daily, such as: the *Manchester Evening News*; the *Evening Standard* (London); the *Belfast Telegraph* and the *Herald* (Glasgow). Others come out weekly, ranging from the *Abergavenny Free Press* to the *Whitby Gazette*, and many of them are freely accessible online. These newspapers will include the whole range of jobs on offer in the locality, not just graduate-only jobs. You'll have to comb through all the ads to check for graduate or direct-entry jobs, but this will give you a good overview of the labour market conditions in that area. If you are keen to live in a particular location, this actually could work to your advantage, because it will make you look at non-graduate jobs as well, and tell you about jobs in that area. So you could always apply for that kind of job to get you to the place you want to be and, once there, start looking for the perfect job for you.

brilliant tip

Quality newspapers offer very good student discounts; just go online to get the vouchers. Not only will you get regular access to job ads, you'll also develop a good habit of serious reading.

Vacancy bulletins and directories

Some publications are devoted entirely to advertising vacancies. They are probably published less frequently than newspapers. There are several produced by Graduate Prospects which are aimed specifically at graduates, and free copies should be available at your university careers service. One example is *Real Prospects Directory* – a comprehensive directory of both graduate recruiters and job opportunities written specifically for students in the final year of their degree. It is produced annually in October. The *Finalist* is a magazine with job vacancies, again aimed at final-year students, and published three times a year in October, January and April.

Specialist bulletins and directories

As well as these two general publications, there are also specialist ones such as *Law*, which lists training contracts and law course vacancies for both law and non-law students. It is an annual publication that appears in September.

Postgraduate bulletins and directories

There are several specialist directories for postgraduate opportunities, including the *Postgraduate Directory*, which includes everything you could want to know about postgraduate courses and opportunities. The *Postgraduate Magazine* covers the same ground, but is published three times a year, in autumn, spring and summer. The *MBA Directory* restricts itself to Master in Business Administration programmes; and finally, the *Funding Guide* (published annually in September) is definitely one you'll need if you intend to continue your studies to postgraduate level.

Directory of work experience and internships for non-finalists

No need to feel left out if you're not yet in your final year. There is one annual publication aimed at non-finalists: *Work Experience and Internships*, that comes out in October.

brilliant tip

Your university careers service should have free copies of these directories and vacancy bulletins, or you can access the digital editions online at **www.prospects.ac.uk**.

Vacancies online

Posting job vacancies online is increasingly common. To find them, you simply need to go online and start looking. You'll find plenty of employers advertising direct to online jobsites. Or perhaps their newspaper advert is made accessible online by the newspaper in question. There are also employment agencies that work on behalf of a range of employers, which means that they might be comprehensive (e.g. **www.monster.co.uk**) or specialised by: occupational sector, such as healthcare and medical jobs (e.g. **www.healthcare.jobs.com**); jobs in the financial sector (e.g. **www.roberthalf.co.uk**); by restricted entry (e.g. **www.thegraduate.co.uk**); or by geography such as jobs in Italy (e.g. **www.italialavoro.net**). Certainly, if you are looking for a job outside the UK, online searches are probably the easiest way to access vacancies. Jobcentre online is the official government jobsite (**www.jobcentreonline.com**) and is searchable by region, industry or company. Some big employers may have their own vacancy web pages such as the NHS (**www.jobs.nhs.uk**). Graduate Prospects is the best-known graduate careers website and is pretty comprehensive, but there are other websites that specialise in graduate recruitment, including **www.milkround.com** and **www.gradunet.co.uk**.

 **tip**

Include new information and communication technologies in your jobsearch. Recruiters make use of any medium that is cost effective, so don't rule any out.

Print vacancies accessible online

The distinction between print and online is increasingly blurred. For example, many newspapers run their advertised vacancies online, and actually make this a selling point when persuading employers to advertise with them. As a jobseeker, this is useful if you forget to check a specific newspaper on a particular day, if you overlooked a vacancy, or if you don't want to buy all the papers every day.

Many of the *Prospects* publications listed earlier in this chapter (see 'Vacancies in print' on p.6) are also available online and are, in some cases, free to download.

Choose a handful of online sites and limit yourself to those for a couple of weeks. You can always change your choice of sites if you're not getting the leads you want from the sites you have chosen; and consider setting up RSS feeds (see below) so that you only get the vacancies you have set parameters for – more on this later in the chapter.

Online vacancies: is more necessarily better?

There is no doubt that by advertising a vacancy online an employer can reach a far greater pool of potential applicants. What is more doubtful is whether the greater pool will necessarily have greater talent. The same goes for you as the jobseeker. By browsing online, you can easily access thousands of job vacancies. In one way, this is great, but you will need to narrow this choice down so you find the kind of job you want, and the kind of job you are a suitable candidate for. Without some kind of filtering mechanism, you could waste a lot of time looking at irrelevant jobs, and you could waste even more time applying for jobs without really thinking. You might even find that you are overwhelmed by the sheer volume of vacancies advertised online and that you become stuck, not knowing how to deal with them all. You do need to have a look at these websites and get a feel for what they offer and how they work. Then you need to make them work for you by being selective.

 **timesaver**

Actively manage your online jobsearch: set filters and review your website choices regularly. Allocate a specific, limited time for checking vacancies online.

RSS feeds: saving you time

If you find a vacancy website that you like, instead of you continually going back and checking that website for updates, you can set up an RSS feed. There are different interpretations of what RSS stands for, but a widely accepted version is the Really Simple Syndication. The feed is basically a bite-sized summary of what's new on that website. Obviously, this saves you time because you don't have to visit each website individually to see what has been updated.

Setting up the feeds

To set up an RSS feed, you are going to need an RSS reader. This is basically a piece of software that checks web pages for updates. Different RSS readers are available for different platforms, so you will need to choose one that works with your computer. An RSS reader can be: web-based, desktop-based or mobile device-based. A web (or browser)-based RSS lets you catch up with your RSS subscriptions from any computer, so has the great advantage of not tying you to a specific computer.

Subscribing to feeds

Having signed up for a web-based RSS reader, first you will need to find sites that syndicate their content, and then subscribe to the feeds you want. You install your reader, add the URL of the feed that you want, then sit back and let the feed come to you. As vacancy sites really want people to see what they have to offer, many are geared up to make an RSS feed as easy to use as possible. You might like to go to the Graduate Prospects site to get you started (**www.prospects.ac.uk**).

brilliant timesaver

Install a web-based RSS feeder, subscribe to feeds from online vacancy sites, then let the updates come to you.

Networking or word of mouth

Why network?

You'll hear a lot about networking within the context of jobsearch in particular and business in general. There is no doubt that networking is important and, in some occupational sectors, it is vital. Take, for example, the University of the Arts London (UAL), whose courses include Art, Fashion, Jewellery and many more. UAL reported that, of the students who graduated in 2009 and found jobs, 80 per cent found their employment through existing networks. Let's try to put that figure in context. This applies only to those students who were employed, and many of the UAL graduates will opt for self-employment. Many UAL graduates move into the creative industries, where contacts and networks are very important in gaining and securing work. Nevertheless, this is a very high percentage, and shows to what extent networking can keep the labour market moving.

▶ brilliant example

'During my internship, I was invited to an event with the then Shadow Home Secretary (Chris Grayling). Quivering like a nervous wreck, I shook his hand, and could barely speak . . . I felt so inferior and out of my depth. I plucked up the courage to ask a question . . . but could literally barely speak I was that nervous. Six months on, we visited a local homeless charity. Chris Grayling arrived . . . he recalled my question from six months back. I realised afterwards the huge difference in my demeanour from our previous encounter.'

Kevin, BSc (Hons) Politics.

Networking in principle

In essence, when you network you take a conscious decision to make the most of every new contact you make, and you treat every single encounter as a possible job lead. You aren't asking them directly for a job, you are simply making them aware that you exist, and that you are the kind of person anyone would want to have working with them. So, no matter how unlikely it may seem, or how remote the chances are of getting a job opening from a random encounter, you work on the principle that every lead could be the one that takes you further towards your brilliant career. Unfortunately, there is no set formula that determines how many contacts equal a job lead. You simply have to be on the alert and be ready to present yourself as a possible employee at any time.

 **brilliant** tip

When you network, you aren't asking directly for a job, you are simply making people aware that you exist, and are the kind of person anyone would like to work with. Just by introducing yourself you show that you are confident, so – go and say hello!

Networking in practice

Graduate job fairs

You may be invited to network in a formal, organised way: graduate job fairs, for example. A graduate fair brings together graduate recruiters, employment professionals and graduate jobseekers. A fair may be generalist (covering all aspects of graduate employment) or specialist (by region or occupational area). It gives you the chance to meet people, and for people to meet you. It makes sense to treat a job fair as a possible recruitment opportunity, so think about how you want to appear. For example, in thinking about what to wear, you might choose something that is more formal than informal. So, without going all out for the power suit, perhaps wear trousers rather than jeans, shirt rather than tee-shirt, and go for something clean and ironed rather than something grubby and creased. You might also like to think about taking some copies of your CV, just in case the opportunity to give it to an employer arises. You may also want to take note of contact details; a notebook is fine for this, but if you do take notes on your phone, make sure you've turned the sound off and do not be tempted to make personal calls when you're on display.

brilliant tip

Make sure your mobile is switched off when you are at a job fair. Potential employers are interested in you, not your ringtone.

Alumni or invited speaker events

There may be alumni events at your university, to which you as a student, may be invited. Alumni means people who have already graduated from your university. Sometimes the alumni events are social, but sometimes they are set up for students to make contacts. The big advantage of talking to alumni is that you already have something in common: your university! And, although they may not have a job opening right now, they may at some point in the future have a vacancy they need to fill, and they may remember meeting you. It may be hard for you to believe it when you meet them, but they too were once a student, just like you, so take the plunge and introduce yourself. Invited speaker events usually involve representatives of particular job areas. They may be in a position to recruit themselves, they may have their own story to share and to inspire you, or they may offer some useful advice. You'll only know what you can get out of it by going to hear them.

brilliant Networking dos and don'ts

Do

✔ treat every encounter as a possible lead;

✔ be polite and pleasant to everyone at all times;

✔ be prepared to ask questions as much as answering them;

✔ follow up any leads promptly: send a message or email the next day at the very latest.

Don't

✘ be intimidated: even if it is a disaster the first time, you'll get better with practice;

✘ be casual: don't chew gum, swear or make phone calls;

✘ get disheartened: if you have nothing concrete to show for an hour of networking, at the very least you have made an effort;

✘ monopolise a contact: let other people get access too.

Networking online

The Internet offers unprecedented possibilities of making yourself known to a very wide audience; and these possibilities can work for you or against you. It is possible to find job opportunities and useful leads through your online presence. However, once you have an online presence, it can be readily accessed by your employer or potential employer – who could think the less of you for having seen uncensored comments or images on your page.

You can establish a presence online by: creating a website or a blog; opening a Twitter account; or joining a social network such as Facebook or LinkedIn. You may be asking yourself whether you need to go online to network but, before we address that question, let's run through the online options.

Websites and blogs

Setting up your own web page allows you to showcase who you are and what you can do. In some sectors it is a very good idea to have a web page. The creative industries, for example: if you are looking for a job in design, it is really important that an employer can view your work. This applies as much to a web designer as to a jewellery designer. The web page then functions as a sort of portfolio that can be accessed by anyone at any time.

A blog (the term is a contracted form of web log) is also a type of web page, but with the explicit intention of charting what has been happening. It allows you to update easily, and should really be updated regularly as an out-of-date blog creates a bad impression. Again, a blog can show what you are capable of, and what you have been doing.

 **tip**

If you have an online presence, keep it up to date. Perhaps not daily but certainly on a regular basis and at least every week.

Forums

A forum may be set up on a website or blog so that the online readers can share responses and ideas on a particular theme. They allow you to express your opinions without necessarily committing to regular input. They also allow you to see what other people are thinking, which might help you to work through a particular issue or challenge. You yourself can use a forum to pose a question and this can be a good way to get into a challenge or problem when you feel really stuck and don't have any clear idea of the way forward. Examples might include: what's a telephone interview like? or, what should I wear to the evening meal at an assessment centre? In this way, you are learning from the collective experience and wisdom of others.

Social networks

Social networks are, at heart, online communities. Just like a real community, you join as a newcomer, make friends and then make friends with your friends' friends. You can then chat, share photos, set up meetings, seek advice and do all the things you would do in real time, but online. There is, however, a clear distinction between different types of social network, what they are used for, and how they are viewed.

Drawing the line between personal and business networks

Broadly speaking, the distinction is between social networking for personal reasons (having fun, gossiping, showing off even) and social networking for professional reasons (getting a job, making business contacts, showing off even). The trick is never to confuse the two. This distinction shows up in the way different social networking sites have developed. Facebook, for example, is definitely for having fun and is therefore a personal space. LinkedIn, on the other hand, is a social network that is clearly aimed at the professional and business side. Keep this distinction clear.

 **tip**

Facebook is for fun, LinkedIn is for business. Keep personal and professional quite separate.

Looking at your personal pages from the employer perspective

While your friends might find it funny and endearing to hear about you embarrassing yourself at a party, your employer (or potential employer) may take a very different view. There are more and more cases of employers seeing material that their workers have posted and, as a consequence, taking disciplinary action including dismissal; and this is where the material has been posted in a personal capacity. If you already have a social networking page, you might like to go through it and take down anything that would put you in a bad light if seen by an employer. And before you post anything from now on, ask yourself if you would be happy to put the post in your window, where it could be seen by passersby, friends of the family or people who know you but aren't necessarily your friends.

 **tip**

Review any social network presence you have set up. Ask yourself this: is my online behaviour how I would behave if a potential employer was in the same room?

Twitter

Twitter is also another online social network, but it has the unique selling point of microblogging. As with a blog (or indeed the status aspect of a social network page), people post an update on their page to show what they are doing, what they are thinking, what is happening in their life right now. On Twitter, however, these posts are restricted to a maximum of 140 characters: this makes for microblogs or tweets.

Using Twitter for job opportunities

Twitter can be useful for following people who lead the way in particular industries as you can see what their thinking is and in what direction they, and by extension their work domain, are heading. Twitter can also be a practical source of job vacancies, and employment agencies do post tweets about new vacancies even before the adverts are posted online. Of course, you'll only get a very brief sense of what the vacancy is (because of the restricted length of the tweet) but that might be enough for you to decide whether to follow it up or leave it alone.

Do I really need an online presence?

We know that not all undergraduates are the same; many will be familiar and happy with virtual communities in an online world, others might feel less comfortable, confident or convinced. There is no clear-cut answer about the need to have an online presence. In some industries, it is vital. In others, it is of little consequence. The important thing to know is that you are always in control of what you post. You can choose to have only a professional presence online and you can closely monitor what you post. You could perhaps limit your commitment, by joining a specific forum to add your voice to a particular debate, or using Twitter just to follow a particular person in a field that interests you. It is probably wise to use online networking, even to a limited extent, and for a limited time, because it does show that you are willing to embrace the new and maybe even to come out of your comfort zone.

 **tip**

If you don't want to commit to a permanent online presence, just contribute to a one-off forum or follow someone on Twitter. Come out of your comfort zone and show you can take on a new challenge.

Speculative applications

Speculative applications (sometimes called applying on spec.) are where you take the initiative and approach an employer to see if there is a possible vacancy, rather than responding to a vacancy once it is advertised. You can of course make speculative applications in a range of media: in person; by email; online; by post. You can waste a lot of time (both yours and also the employer's time) in sending off speculative applications that have no chance of success. And you can feel a lot of rejection if the speculative applications you send out get you nowhere, not even a response. But speculative applications do work, especially in very niche areas. Take a look at our brilliant example, in which Oliver's first job as a junior engineer pays very little, but gives him valuable experience which he uses to secure a better job not once but twice in a row: a brilliant example of leverage in the labour market, as well as speculative applications.

▶ brilliant example

'When a new Formula One team was starting up for the following season, I saw an opportunity and speculatively applied for a position. Luckily they saw potential in me, and recognised my experience and qualifications. I spent two-and-a-half years at this Formula One team as a systems engineer on the race team, until they had to withdraw from racing due to financial reasons . . . due to contacts I had gained in the industry, I quickly secured employment with a motorsports electronics company, providing hardware and services to the governing body of motorsport.'

Oliver, ME (Civil), MSc Motorsport Engineering and Management

Focusing your speculative approach

It is important to invest time before you send a speculative application. You'll need to know the market, be clear who are the relevant employers, and have a very good understanding of what their business needs. With a speculative application, you are basically offering your blend of skills and know-how as the solution to a staffing problem the employer hasn't really worked out yet. Online research can really help you here: to look at the individual employer and to put that employer in the overall context of the current market. Networking also plays a strong part, as you identify who to approach, and you approach people who may have some idea of who you are either from a previous encounter or by recommendation.

 **example**

'I started off looking for a job on the Mediterranean coast because I'd got the chance of accommodation there. So basically I got a load of CVs and went round pretty much every restaurant, because that was where I had most experience . . . it was horrible, really scary because I didn't really know what I was saying (in French). One place phoned back, invited me for an interview, and gave me a job as a runner.'

Hannah, (undergraduate) Economics and Politics with International Studies

Self-employment

You might like to consider creating your own job vacancy by working for yourself. Self-employment is quite common in some sectors, notably the creative industries. However, it can also work in less obvious occupational areas: for example, counselling or computer programming. It will involve a lot of hard work, but it can be very rewarding to shape your own destiny, and to make your first million. You will need to come up with a business idea, and you will need to develop a business plan. Your own university might offer courses in self-employment, or should be able to signpost you to other sources of help. The local jobcentre should be able to point you to sources of advice and often local authorities (the local council) promote and support new businesses. You could perhaps talk to your bank to see what support they can offer: they should be able to give you some idea of what a business plan involves and may even offer access to a business advisor. Networking can really help you here: you can ask successful entrepreneurs how they have achieved their success, and you can ask around for tips and advice from people who have taken this path. You don't even need to do it in person: social networking is perfect for this kind of exploration.

brilliant tip

Make the most of help on offer for a business start-up. This includes help targeted at graduates. Banks can offer useful information, as can jobcentres.

Dimensions: of time, of geography, of chance

The time dimension: watch out for closing dates

A daily newspaper will carry vacancies for which the closing date is likely to be a couple of weeks; in a magazine published less frequently, the vacancies will be around for longer; and in the annual directories, the publication of the directory may happen some months before the closing date. Don't be lulled into a false sense of security here: although there may well be a rolling programme of recruitment, it is nearly always better to apply sooner rather than later.

The geographical dimension: working where *you* want to work

The geographical reach of jobsearch can also vary from local through regional and national to European or global. This applies equally to both sides of the market: you might be looking very widely, and the employer may also be putting a vacancy out into the marketplace at different levels. At the most local level, they can simply put up a notice in the workplace. Typically, this would be in a shop window, just saying something like: VACANCY – ENQUIRE WITHIN. A wider local search would be through local newspapers, the weekly paid or freesheets. Regional search would use daily regional newspapers or local radio. There could even be a regional website advertising, for example, jobs in the North West of England, or a job fair that also covers a regional area. A nationwide approach would use national daily or weekend papers, or websites: these could also be used for global search.

brilliant tip

If you are keen to work in a particular location, try looking at a local paper or vacancy publication in that area. You could even walk around the area and see what kind of employers there are, and then send speculative applications to them.

The chance dimension (sometimes called serendipity)

Sometimes it looks like some people just get lucky: everything comes together and they are in the right place, at the right time, with the right skills for the right job. It can happen like that and, without making any great effort, somebody gets lucky and a job falls into their lap. If you see that happen for someone else, you might be tempted to wait around in the hope that the job fairy will come to your rescue. Or you can start to create your own luck. Because often, much, much more often, things come together after a lot of hard work. Without that hard work, the individual elements would not be ready to come together.

 **brilliant** tip

If you aren't making progress in your jobsearch, try another approach. Think laterally, be resourceful and use the full range of possibilities presented in this chapter.

Creating your own luck

So what can you do to get everything in place? Well, you need to ensure that you have developed the necessary skills and know-how. Chapter 2 'The graduate labour market' takes you through the skills employers are looking for, and Chapter 8 'Work experience; making it purposeful' shows you how to develop your range of desirable skills through purposeful work experience. You also need to ensure that you are ready to respond quickly to a job possibility, by having your CV up to date, perhaps having a completed job application form you can adapt to a new vacancy. Chapter 10 'Making applications: getting past the first post' takes you through all these processes and more. Fundamentally, to get a job you have to be in the job market, and employers have to know that you are in the market for their job. It goes right back to the opening of this chapter: for the market to work, supply (you) and demand (employers) have to know about each other.

 **brilliant** recap

- Look at vacancies from the employer's perspective.

- Use printed media: directories, newspapers, magazines.

- Use online media: online newspapers and websites.

- Look widely to check what's out there, then narrow your search so you aren't wasting your (or the employer's time) with unfocused applications.

- Use timesaving devices: filters, alerts, Twitter, RSS feeds.

- Get networking: job fairs, alumni events, contacts – treat every encounter as a possible step forward towards your job.

- Use social networks, but review your online presence to ensure you present online at all times as a serious contender for a job opening.

- Consider the option of self-employment: take up any help on offer.

- Give the Job Fairy a helping hand by doing everything you can to create your own luck.

What to do next

Check out the demand side of the labour market

If you are thinking about what to do next, you could take one step towards checking out what is in demand in the job market by picking up a quality newspaper (*Guardian, Independent, Daily Telegraph, The Times*) to look at the job vacancies advertised there. Go online, visit a few of the job websites we have included in this chapter. While you're there, try setting up an RSS feed so the jobs adverts come to you.

Make your presence known in the supply side of the labour market

You could take one step towards making your presence (as a jobseeker) known in the job market, by checking if your university is running a job fair – and, if they are, go along to it. Tell people that you are actively seeking work. Think about posting your CV online on one of the job websites. Ideally, you should cover both sides of the job market: checking out the demand side, and making your presence known on the supply side.

CHAPTER 2

The graduate labour market

Increasingly, employers will look for some more interesting skills; things like cultural sensitivity and what makes a global graduate. Sometimes you have to go sideways to get to where you want to be.

Carl Gilleard, Chief Executive, Association of Graduate Recruiters

This chapter will help you to make sense of the graduate labour market. You are going to need to understand how the labour market works if you are to find your way around it – which you need to do as you work towards securing your brilliant career. You need to know that the labour market is both complex and dynamic. This is the chapter you are most likely to turn to when riffling through this book, and it is probably the most difficult chapter to write. Difficult to write firstly, because we want to present some fairly complex concepts in a very accessible way. That's because you are going to need an understanding of how the labour market works if you are to find your way around it, which you need to do as you work towards securing your brilliant career. Difficult secondly, because any labour market is not only complex, but also dynamic: it doesn't stand still but constantly shifts and changes in response to a range of factors which shape the supply of and demand for workers. That dynamism means that you may want to consult some online sources of up-to-the-minute data if you want a real-time assessment of what's going on in the graduate labour market when you actually read this.

So this chapter is going to take you through some key concepts in employment, then it will look at why employers want graduates and what graduates have to offer in terms of knowledge, skills and abilities. We will also look at small to medium-sized enterprises (SMEs) as these play a significant role in graduate recruitment, but can be overlooked by graduate jobseekers. We then have a brief overview of what kind of employment sectors graduates have gone into in recent years and the kind of wages they start out with.

 **tip**

The labour market is constantly changing but you can easily get the most up-to-date information online.

Fundamentals of the labour market: supply and demand

There are two sides to any market, and that includes the labour market

You'll hear talk of 'the labour market' when issues of employment, unemployment, job vacancies and employability are discussed. 'Labour' here means simply to do with work. The term 'labour market' is used to describe the interactions between employers who need labour (or workers, to put it another way) and employees (those who can supply that labour or undertake that work). The study of the labour market is of interest to economists, and can be seen as a discipline in itself. Understanding how the labour market works and keeping up to date with what's happening with job vacancies and demands is important for careers advisers too.

Picture a market in your mind's eye

The idea of a 'market' helps us to envisage what is going on. So just take a moment to think of a market (or supermarket or shop) from your own experience. It might be a bustling, chaotic place with people shouting out what they are hoping to sell – or it might be extremely organised into tidy aisles stacked full of goods with special offer stickers pointing out the best buys.

You are the 'supply' in the graduate labour market

Whatever the setting, there are always two sides in play. On the one hand, there are people offering goods for sale (goods such as a pair of trainers or a bunch of grapes); on the other, people who are looking to buy what's on offer. And that's the first key point: for the market to work, you have to have supply (stuff being offered) and demand (stuff being wanted). Don't be insulted if we now compare you to a pair of trainers or a bunch of grapes, but you are the supply in the labour market. You are available, on show, ready to be snapped up by someone with money to secure you – and a discerning eye to know a quality product (be it trainers, grapes or graduates) when it's up for grabs.

 **definitions**

The term **supply** refers to all the people who are actively seeking work – which of course includes you.

The term **demand** refers to all the jobs that are looking to be filled – which is, of course, what you want.

The relationship between supply and demand is critical in your jobsearch

It is clear that 'supply' and 'demand' are the two fundamental forces driving the labour market. So the relationship between supply and demand is critical. As you are part of the supply side, it is important that you think about the market from the other perspective and get a sense of how employers work and what kind of supply they are looking for (demanding). This allows you to tailor your offer (of yourself for hire) to their demand. That could be a relatively simple task: presenting your skills, knowledge and understanding in a way that makes it easy for an employer to understand exactly what you have to offer and how that fits with what they need in their workforce. Have a look at Chapter 10 for advice on making sure that your application gets past the first post. It could, however, require a complex, more lengthy task which might be that you seek to expand your skills, knowledge and understanding (that is, working on expanding your professional repertoire) by undertaking voluntary work or work shadowing, or accepting a job that you don't really want to do now in order to get the job you want in the future: your brilliant career.

brilliant tip

When you are looking for a job, so that you present what you have to offer in a way that the employer will easily recognise, try to think from the employer's perspective. Look at what they want and why they want it. Then make sure that you've got what they want and you showcase that in your application.

What's distinctive about the graduate labour market?

Graduate labour as a distinct sector within the labour market

You may be wondering why graduates are treated as a distinct subgroup within the labour market. Defining sectors is just a way of examining the labour market in more detail, and is helpful in getting a hold on labour market information which could otherwise be unwieldy and overwhelming. Market analysts often drill into data so that they can get the low-down on a particular sector. A sector can be defined by occupation (e.g. Engineering or Business or Creative Arts) or by geography (the South East or Greater Merseyside) or by shared characteristics of the workforce (graduates). We'll look at occupational sectors in more detail in Chapter 3 'Labour market information: analysis of what graduates do', but for now we'll look at the graduate labour market: which simply means that the demand is for graduate level jobs, for which the jobseeker (the supply) must have an undergraduate degree (at least).

brilliant definition

The labour market can be subdivided into **sectors**, which makes it easier to focus. These **sectors** can be defined by occupational grouping, by geographical territory, or by shared characteristics of the workforce, such as being a graduate.

What work do graduates actually do?

Every year the Higher Education Statistics Agency (HESA) asks graduates to report what they have gone on to do after they finished their degree. A questionnaire goes out to all those finishing an undergraduate degree, which includes Foundation degrees. It only goes to people who are resident in the United Kingdom or the European Union, so does not include postgraduates or overseas students who are not UK residents. It only asks about their 'first' destination: that is, what they were doing six months after completing their degree. Destinations include: work (paid employment); further study (perhaps at postgraduate level); looking for work; and not available for work (e.g. travelling). Chapter 3 'Labour market information: analysis of what graduates do' goes into some detail about what graduates from different degrees go on to do. This makes it easy for you to check where people who did the same degree as you ended up. The results are presented by broad subject area (e.g. Social Sciences) then broken down into its particular disciplines (for Social Sciences this would include Economics and Sociology).

Graduate earnings

One noticeable characteristic of the graduate labour market is that wages are higher. Of course, it is perfectly possible to earn higher than average earnings without a degree, where your skills and talents are in demand. This is particularly true where the supply of skill is very limited, so employers are competing with each other to secure the services of a limited pool of talent. These highly sought-after skills come at a premium, which means the employers have to pay more. A classic example here would be a footballer: the employer's primary concern is ability as a footballer, not the level of formal education achieved. However, if you look at graduates in the labour market as a whole and compare their lifetime earnings, on average graduates earn more than non-graduates. A worker with a first degree (that is an undergraduate degree) earns between 20–25 per cent more than a worker with 2 A levels (or equivalent). That can work out to £160,000 more over the course of a whole working life. This is often referred to as the 'graduate premium'. These are only averages, and the actual earnings of any individual graduate can vary considerably from this average figure. The degree subject you take, the job you go into, the kind of employer you work for and the location of your employment will all have a bearing on your earnings over your lifetime.

Is the graduate premium guaranteed?

As the number of graduates entering the labour market increases, and if the number of graduate jobs on offer decreases, the 'graduate premium' may diminish. But we will know this only once we have tracked more recent graduates over time so we can take a long-term perspective: data that we simply can't get until time elapses. Nevertheless, from the data currently available (from a government report on fair access to the professions) there are clear economic benefits to having a degree. This may not ring true if you are battling through difficult economic times when graduate jobs are hard fought and hard won. It may be difficult to think about this now, or to believe that it's important, but when you get towards retirement age you will look back and see what a difference having a degree has made in the long run.

brilliant definition

The **graduate premium**, in labour market terms, is the difference in earnings potential for graduates as a sector of the market compared with other groups of workers. The graduate premium requires employers to pay higher wages to secure a graduate to fill their vacancy. The graduate premium means that graduate earnings over a lifetime are likely to be higher than for non-graduates.

How graduates differ from other occupational sectors

There are a couple of other significant differences when you compare graduates in the labour market with other groups of workers.

They are more mobile in the labour market, which means that they are more likely to move to another part of the country to take up work and may even work outside their country of origin. Employers are also more likely to move their graduate workers about, though will often offer incentives and rewards for doing so.

Another, curious characteristic is that graduates are more likely to be given further training. This can often be in-house or on-the-job training, but can also mean sending graduate workers on specialist and/or postgraduate courses at universities.

 Most graduates now are expected to do regular evaluations of where they are at and where they are going . . . developing the individual to the point where they can take control of their life, their learning and their career.

Carl Gilleard, Chief Exectuive, Association of Graduate Recruiters

It may seem odd that employers want their skilled people to get even more skilled – but they know that graduates can learn (see below) and a more highly skilled worker is more highly prized because they can do more. The flip side of being offered this kind of opportunity is that employers expect their graduate workers to progress in their careers and invest in their own professional development. Of course, expanding your professional repertoire in this way benefits you because it gives you more leverage in the labour market.

Not all graduates are the same

 **example**

'My last job was a stop-gap really: it wasn't the job I wanted and it wasn't the money I wanted. But I wanted to learn, I was interested and, gradually, it built. The longer I was there, the more things were handed over. So then when it came to the pay review I could say: "I'm doing this now, and I want to be paid for it." I'd proved myself. After five years, I was earning nearly three times the salary I started on.'

Sophie, employee in small to medium-sized enterprise

brilliant **example**

'I was a (very) mature student, already in my chosen career as a mental health recovery and rehabilitation worker. I decided to study Psychology for several reasons: I enjoyed it at A level, I never had the chance to go to university when I left school and wondered if I could do it, and the subject is closely linked to my work . . . I have much more confidence in decision making and suggestions I make at work now. I feel the knowledge I now have of theories and empirical evidence . . . enhances the experience I already had.'

Linda, BSc (Hons) Psychology

We have been talking of a graduate labour market as if all graduates are the same, but that's clearly nonsense. Graduates are different, one from the other, because people are different. Two students may be studying on the same programme, even in the same tutor group, and yet hold very different values and so will be looking for jobs in distinctly different ways. One may be highly motivated by money; the other by job satisfaction and a work–life balance. One may be happy to relocate from one place of work to another within an organisation, or even to move from one country to another if their employer demands it or if a good job offer comes up. For other graduates, family responsibilities, emotional ties or just a strong sense of belonging may keep them in one place, and so they may restrict their jobsearch to a particular geographical area. Some graduates are changing career direction completely and have retrained in order to step out in a completely new career direction. Others will be starting out and their first graduate job may well be their first job. Some graduates will hold out for the job that matches their specification of a dream job. For others, any job will do: they just need to earn money to live. So, even though this chapter treats graduates as a set of workers sharing graduate-level qualifications, there are huge differences for individuals, who will make their own decisions and carve their own path to what is a brilliant career, for them.

 **recap**

- As a group, graduates earn more over the course of their working life than non-graduates.

- Graduate workers tend to move location and/or employer more than non-graduates.

- Graduates undertake more training and personal development than other workers.

- Employers will pay a premium for highly skilled workers, especially if supply is limited.

- All graduates are individuals who will carve out their own brilliant career.

What's distinctive about graduates as a labour supply?

Why would employers pay more for a graduate?

So why are employers prepared to pay more for workers who have a degree? Graduate employees tend to bring innovation and creativity to their work, which solves business problems and can increase productivity. That's not to say that other groups of workers don't do that but graduates, as a workforce and on the whole, have a proven track record for doing so. Broadly speaking, graduates are paid to think, so they add value to their work, which in turn adds value to the organisation they work for, which in turn repays the 'graduate premium'.

How do employers know what graduates are capable of?

You might think that employers are just taking it on trust that graduates can think, and will be able to apply intellectual and cognitive abilities. Well, yes and no. Employers can take it on trust, because there are clear standards of achievement that are expected before a student can be awarded a degree. Although individual universities award their own degrees, all degrees in England, Wales and Northern Ireland work to the framework for higher education qualifications published by the Quality Assurance Agency for Higher Education. The framework sets the benchmark for what graduates should achieve in their degree, whether Foundation, Honours or Masters.

brilliant tip

As a graduate, you are trained to think: to think critically, to think creatively, to think things through. You need to show an employer how your training in thinking can benefit their organisation or add value to their enterprise.

What graduates should be able to do

For example, on successful completion of their programme, an Honours graduate should be able to:

- understand key aspects of their field of study (including coherent and detailed knowledge);
- conduct analysis and enquiry; devise and sustain arguments, and/or solve problems;
- appreciate uncertainty and ambiguity; and
- manage their own learning.

What graduates are able to do from the employer's perspective

All of these competencies would relate primarily to the subject or discipline you are studying, whether that is Fine Art, Computer Science or Medicine. From an employer's point of view, that ability to think transfers into the workplace as:

- the exercise of initiative and personal responsibility;

- decision making in complex and unpredictable contexts;

- effective communication of information, ideas, problems and solutions to specialist and non-specialist audiences; and

- the learning ability needed to undertake appropriate further training of a professional or equivalent nature.

So, when an employer specifically advertises a graduate job, and demands that their employee has a first degree, they expect graduate employees to work at this level of sophistication in their workplace.

How employers view subject discipline

Between 50 and 60 per cent of graduate jobs advertised don't specify the degree discipline – which means you can apply no matter what subject you studied. This statistic has remained fairly constant for a long time, so we can assume that it will hold good for some time to come. What it tells us is that it is your thinking power that employers want, not necessarily the specialist knowledge of your discipline. You might have to help the employer recognise that, despite you studying a very different subject from them, you have got what they are looking for. (Of course, where an employer wants a specialist, such as a doctor, lawyer, dentist or graphic designer, then they will advertise specifically for those roles and qualifications. This accounts for about half the graduate jobs advertised.) The important thing here is to remember to look at things from the employer's perspective. You might well have a degree in a subject about which the employer knows nothing at all. This could be anything, from Classical Civilisation to Sports and Exercise Studies. The employer may even have preconceptions about your degree, thinking, for example, that Arts and Design graduates don't have any commercial understanding, or not realising that Psychology requires a good understanding of statistics. So you may well have to scrutinise your skills and experience and present what you know in a way that the employer can't fail to grasp. What you can know for sure is that, if you have achieved an undergraduate degree, you have proven thinking power – and that is in demand.

 **tip**

About half of the graduate vacancies on offer do not specify a particular degree discipline. So you can broaden your jobsearch beyond your field of study.

Not all employers are big organisations

 **example**

'I've worked in SMEs for several years now. It's actually far more challenging working for a smaller company than it is working for a larger company. You have more opportunity to shine, in fact, and to move up quickly.'

Sophie, Evotel Holdings employee

Why are small to medium-sized enterprises important?

SMEs play a huge part in the economy: in the EU, 99 per cent of all enterprises are SMEs. In the UK, annual data published by the Department of Business and Skills (BIS, 2010) shows that SMEs accounted for 99.9 per cent of all enterprises and 59.8 per cent of private-sector employment. That means a lot of people are actually working in SMEs (13.6 million at the last count) and that includes graduates. The turnover of SMEs was 5.8 per cent higher in 2009 compared with 2008, which means that there are opportunities for employment in SMEs. Now do you see why they are so important?

 **example**

Evotel Holdings supplies televisions to electrical retailers in the United Kingdom. They import televisions and they import components which are assembled in the UK and in the European Union. They are in a network of repair agents, working for manufacturers, insurers and retailers. Their market is characterised by high volume and low margin, which means very little tolerance if they are to make a profit. They must deliver on quality, on quantity and on time. A successful small to medium-sized enterprise, Evotel has to stay smart to keep ahead of its competitors.

What is an SME?

SMEs are vital to the economy, both in the United Kingdom and throughout Europe. But what exactly is an SME? The letters simply stand for small to medium-sized enterprise, but we need to define these terms too in order to understand what an SME is.

What is an enterprise?

There is no one definition, but in economic terms, an enterprise is an organisation created for business venture. So an organisation intends to do business and preferably to do business that makes a profit.

Small, medium-sized – or micro?

The size of an enterprise can be determined either by the number of people or the amount of money involved. The technical terms here are headcount or turnover/balance sheet total. From an employment perspective it is probably easier to think in terms of how many people are involved in the business: the headcount. In a headcount, no distinction is made between full-time and part-time workers: so if an SME has five full-time and five part-time, that makes ten workers. In the EU, the headcount includes employees and self-employed people working in the enterprise. Whereas in the UK, the headcount applies only to employees (BIS, 2010). But both the EU and the UK agree the headcount categories for SMEs, which are as follows:

micro = headcount up to 10

small = headcount of at least 10 and up to 50

medium-sized = headcount of more than 50, up to 250

Although we often think of SMEs as small, they can actually be very small indeed, or quite sizeable. They can often be overlooked because the individual enterprises aren't household names. However, the opportunities in SMEs are statistically significant, and certainly worth investigating.

 **tip**

Include SMEs in your jobsearch. You may not have heard their name, but they are a powerful force in the labour market. They are less likely to spend much money on advertising, so do your research and consider making a speculative application to a targeted SME. They really don't have any time to waste, so make sure you focus your application.

What to do next

There is every chance that you know someone who works for an SME – why not ask them about their work and their workplace? It would be interesting to see if they felt they had had any particular opportunities because of the small scale of their employment – or if they perceived any disadvantage.

Graduates need employability skills

What employers want: skillset and mindset

Having said that graduates are in demand in the labour market because of their proven ability to think, and having shown that employers pay a 'graduate premium', graduates are expected to offer more than their intellect: all graduates need good employability skills. This message comes through loud and clear from employers responding to a joint survey run by the Confederation of British Industry (CBI) and Universities UK. Now, there is no one agreed definitive list of employability skills – there isn't even one agreed term. Sometimes these skills are called 'soft skills' or 'transferable skills' as well as 'employability skills'.

It is interesting to look at these terms in turn because they give an insight into what is in demand in the labour market, which allows you to pinpoint what you, as the supply, can offer or may need to develop. There is growing evidence that employers also value mindset. This refers to a set of attitudes and behaviours that allow workers to add value to their employing organisation. Some of these attitudes benefit the employee just as much as the employer: taking pride in your work and giving your best makes for greater satisfaction and self-esteem – both key in positive psychology.

 The graduates we employ are over-qualified for work in the warehouse or the call centre. But we employ graduates because they're more attentive, more willing to do a proper day's work. You have to assume they've got the ability to do the job, but if they haven't got it 100 per cent, it's not going to take us long to train them.

Julian Radley, Director, Evotel Holdings

Hard skills refer to such abilities as numeracy and literacy, managing a project or working in a team. It is relatively easy for an employer to check that you have them (have a look at Chapter 11 for more on what kind of selection tests are used and how best to succeed in them). In contrast, soft skills are less easy to test for with any scientific reliability, but they can be observed and demonstrated. So 'soft' here doesn't mean that they are easier skills to acquire, but that they are more difficult to pin down for assessment. Transferable skills mean simply that the skills can be developed in one job and taken with you to another job. A good example here would be customer care.

Customer care means dealing with customers: it involves the ability to listen, to question, to understand the issue, to convey that understanding to a customer (without losing your temper!) and to work towards resolving the issue in hand to the satisfaction of both parties. Customer care is important in a wide variety of contexts: looking after patients in a hospital; dealing with complaints from corporate clients; handling irate customers in a queue or on a shop floor. What the customers/clients/patients are concerned about doesn't matter: your skills and abilities can be used effectively no matter what the context. The transferability of these skills also means that you can develop skills in one aspect of your life that may not necessarily be paid work, and can then use them in your employment. An example of this would be the negotiation skills you have to develop as a parent (particularly of toddlers), which stand you in good stead when negotiating in a work environment.

 **definition**

Employers value a range of behaviours and aptitudes, which can be used in a range of employment contexts. They might be called **transferable**, **soft** or **employability** skills. Their name doesn't matter, but the skills do.

Employability skillset and mindset

Here is our list of employability skills, drawn from a range of sources including the Confederation of British Industries (CBI). As they represent employers, this is very much from the demand perspective. They aren't presented in any particular order, because each of these skills is important in its own right, and different employers will place different emphasis on different skills at different times in the lifecycle of their own business. Although we can't give a precise indicator of demand for each of the skills, in an employer survey undertaken by the CBI, 80 per cent of employers were not satisfied with foreign language fluency, and over a third of employers were not satisfied with graduate levels of business and customer awareness.

 It doesn't matter what the business is, there are some fundamental principles: cash flow is king; you've got to make sure there's a bottom line for the profit; and you've got to look at risk. Graduates need to ask where they fit into the critical path within the business process.

Julian Radley, Director, Evotel Holdings

Self-management

Broadly speaking, self-management is the ability to take responsibility for a role or a given task. If you accept responsibility, then a number of attitudes and behaviours will follow from that. You will probably be prepared to be flexible and you may need to be assertive as and when appropriate. You'll need to be a self-starter, getting on with things and not waiting to be asked or to be directed. You'll also have to be aware of the need to manage your time. A key aspect of self-management is that you are prepared to improve your own performance with every task, role or job that you do. This improvement will come from two complementary perspectives. Firstly, your own reflective practice, where you think about what you've done, what went well and what could be done better next time round. Secondly, feedback from others, which is likely to be a mixture of positive and negative feedback. You will learn, and take the lessons you learn with you, no matter where you go next.

▶ brilliant example

'Aside from academic development, personal skills gained through my time at university are arguably as valuable. I've always been fairly confident, and university life allowed me to understand myself better: my strengths, weaknesses and life goals. Within two months of leaving university (in a very tough economic environment) I had secured a great job. I believe my time at university equipped me with the creative problem-solving skills that I need to excel within my industry – online brand reputation management.

Alex, BA (Hons) Graphic Design

Resilience

Resilience is what sustains you to keep going with a task or responsibility even when the going gets tough and you might be tempted to give up. Resilience requires your commitment to stay involved, some degree of control or influence and a sense of personal challenge to develop. Optimism plays an important part, but it has to be realistic, not hoping for some magic wand you can wave. Knowing what you're feeling and why is also important here, as is the ability to slow down and consider alternatives when you seem to hit a blank wall.

▶ brilliant example

'I was working in France as a runner in a big American-themed sports bar. Although it was an American place, everybody spoke French all the time. I didn't think I was going to take it: it was really busy and I didn't know anyone, not a single person . . . at first it was overwhelming: everyone was older; everyone was French; there was so much to learn, the menu and the ordering, but eventually I made friends and in the end I was sorry to leave.'

Hannah, (undergraduate) Economics and Politics with International Studies

Team-working

This is obviously about working well with others. However, in order to do that you have to be aware that your individual contribution (and success) can be separated out from that of others in your team: you have to be aware of this interdependence and have to be able to manage yourself as a team-worker, not just as an individual. The behaviours that support effective team-working are sharing ideas with others by contributing to discussions and planning, and what follows from that is the need to cooperate with others and to respect them. Negotiating and persuading skills are key here.

▶ brilliant example

'A lot of the course I studied was teamwork-based, which enabled me to increase my confidence in working within a team. We also had to give a lot of presentations, which I found really nerve-racking, but it really did boost my confidence. I actually realised I did have a special talent for talking to groups and this encouraged me to consider teaching as a career.'

Katie, BSc (Hons) Animal Behaviour and Welfare

Business and customer awareness

Although this really is a soft skill, in that you can't necessarily train or test people in it, you can see very clearly when people don't have it. Some employers of graduates say that this is the employability skill most often missing in applicants and new entrants. Although you would expect it to be very much in demand in the retail and business sector, it is actually very important in service and public service sectors too. It means understanding what drives a successful business or service, but that doesn't necessarily mean at the high strategic level. It is very much the bottom-up approach: keeping customers satisfied, understanding why you need to build customer loyalty, understanding how innovation can drive a business forward – and how the lack of innovation can mean a business grinding to a halt. It also includes an appreciation of the need to take calculated risks: not reckless, but bold nonetheless.

 Initiative is an important thing in an employee; but they've got to be aware of what that opportunity is, and when the opportunity comes, and then how to deal with it. We needed some marketing expertise – someone remembered marketing was on Seb's CV, so he got the chance to step up to it.

Julian Radley, Director, Evotel Holdings

Problem solving

Another skill that is pretty obvious, really. It will involve you analysing facts or data, and weighing up the context or situations. You'll need to work creatively, perhaps coming at problems from different angles and looking for a variety of approaches; and in order to solve the problem, you'll need to come up with appropriate solutions. A lot of your undergraduate work gets you to do this kind of thing, even if it isn't immediately obvious: linguists translating unfamiliar phrases need to puzzle things out, not simply reach for the nearest dictionary.

What happens is: we need to do something quickly and the only way
to get someone quickly is to use someone that's here. Suddenly we
realise someone's got more ability than we realised. Spotting talent
is mostly by luck, which I think is wrong; we should be a bit
more observant.

Julian Radley, Director, Evotel Holdings

Project management

This skill is increasingly sought after. As a graduate employee, you may be
asked to manage projects – and you need to be clear that you will probably
be asked to manage more than one project at time. Effective project
management calls on many of the skills listed here: communication and
literacy; team-working; problem solving and resilience. You probably will
have had direct experience of managing a project on your degree – just
think about your final year dissertation or project or end of year show –
and you had to do that while managing other 'projects' – your brilliant
career included.

Communication and literacy

This means the ability to read, write and to get your message across, which
may seem really obvious. You should be able to write clearly and be able to
structure your written work so that it makes sense. You should also be able
to modulate the tone of your work to reach your intended readership. You
should have good communication skills (sometimes called oral literacy),
which means the ability to listen carefully, check your understanding and
question appropriately. Poor communication is one of the greatest sources
of frustration and irritation to employers; yet you can improve on this
every single day, no matter what context you are operating in.

▶ brilliant example

'I completed a foundation degree in animal management. As well as the huge variety of academic knowldge I gained, I also made a lot of personal developments which have really helped boost my confidence. What was particularly useful was the greater understanding of general writing skills I gained, including grammar and written communication. I feel that my academic writing improved over my time at university and, not only did these skills give me further confidence when completing assignments, but these are skills that I can use in any job environment, whatever the sector.'

Jessica, FdSc Animal Management

Numeracy

You do need to get your head around what is understood by numeracy. It does not mean advanced mathematical tasks, but fairly general awareness of the importance of maths as a tool in practical day-to-day work. The confidence to tackle mathematical problems in the workplace is in demand by employers. To dismiss this because you think you can't do Maths is like saying you can't read and write. If you haven't got a formal qualification in maths (such as Maths GCSE grade A*–C or equivalent), you really should think about doing some basic Maths programme so that you aren't cut off from a lot of jobs that need you to have confidence with numbers on a fairly basic level.

Application of Information Technology

This includes a range of Information Technology skills including: word processing; using spreadsheets; setting up and managing files; using email appropriately and using Internet search engines appropriately. As IT applications develop, it is important to keep up: not just in terms of playing with the latest games or applications, but also in terms of how these new ways of working and communicating and problem solving translate into everyday work.

Foreign language skills

This is quite a tricky one to get to the bottom of, but an easy one to dismiss if you think that, if you speak English, you don't need to worry about language competence. Languages are in demand in addition to the skill set outlined above: there are few jobs where language ability on its own is the key demand. The level of language skill can vary: in some cases technical mastery and fluency is called for, but everyday conversational ability can be useful, as can a general awareness of cultural differences. Even having a few key phrases in another language can really pave the way for effective relationships, which are at the heart of any business or dealings.

 **example**

'What's difficult about working abroad? I want to say the language, but it's not that. It's the way of doing things, getting your head around things.'

Hannah, (undergraduate) Economics and Politics with International Studies

Developing employability skills, even when you're not employed

Employers demand that graduates can demonstrate a range of transferable skills which have been shown to enhance their performance in the workplace. This is on top of your degree. The more you develop these employability skills the more attractive you become to an employer, so the greater your chances of success in your jobsearch. It is important to understand that you don't need to be in paid employment to develop all of these skills. For example, if you don't have a job, you can still develop your fluency in a foreign language just by listening to the radio or podcasts in that language, reading an online newspaper or novel, or even watching a film or TV programme. You can develop your customer awareness and business sense just by being aware of what is going on around you: think about how businesses advertise for and treat their customers. What promises do they make about customer service and how do they deliver on that promise?

Observing and analysing behaviours that you come across every day just as a possible customer (not even a consumer) will enhance your understanding. And, of course, if you are struggling to secure a job in a difficult labour market, you are continually practising resilience and self-management; and the real beauty is that, having developed these skills, whether through paid employment, volunteer work or simply on your own, they stick with you and you can use them to move around and progress in the labour market.

brilliant tip

Seek out opportunities to develop employability skills. You can do this in any job at any level. You can also do it through volunteering and even in unpaid work. Keep a record of your skills development to use when applying for jobs.

What do graduates earn?

Data published in 2010 presented the median starting salaries for graduates according to the broad sector of work they went into. These are average salaries, so the range of salary within that particular sector can be a couple of thousand pounds less – or indeed a few thousand pounds more. The salary shown here represents the mid point of all the salaries earned in that sector in that year. The other thing to remember is that these refer to starting salaries: earnings over time can be considerably more, depending of course on the subject studied and the whole package of skills and knowledge and understanding an individual job seeker has to offer.

 The work has changed. When I was a kid you wanted to be a bus driver! You learn there are certain job markets and there needs to be a reality check, to learn what job markets pay.

Julian Radley, Director, Evotel Holdings

The average starting salary for a graduate was £19,675 (£22,228 in London), which obviously means that some sectors, on average, had a higher starting salary and others had a lower average starting salary. In the Sales and Customer Services sector and in the Marketing sector, the average was lower at £18,804. Slightly above that was the Information Technology professional sector, which came in at £22,167. Human Resources as a sector was pitched at the overall average. Scientists had an average salary of £20,539, which may seem low when Science graduates are in demand. We should remember that many professional jobs in Science demand a higher degree, so what we are looking at here is just the average of first destinations, immediately on graduation. Engineers came in a little higher with a sector average starting salary of £23,637, and jobs in the Managerial sector averaged £23,683. It is significant that, in the same survey, two-thirds of the employers who responded reported difficulty filling vacancies in Science, Technology, Engineering and Mathematics (the so-called STEM subject areas). This is significant because, if the demand is greater than the supply, employers have to pay more to secure the workers, and this is reflected in the average starting salary in that sector being higher than for graduate starting salaries taken as a whole. The starting salary for jobs in the Finance sector is high partly because many of those jobs are concentrated in London and the South East, which attract a premium because of higher living costs, but also because some individual salaries can be very high indeed.

Points of entry and points of leverage

Points of entry

It is important here to remember that these are the average starting salaries; that is, the kind of salary you can expect when you are starting out in one of these graduate careers. That starting position is your 'point of entry'. In a survey of 16,000 undergraduates in their final year (they were due to graduate in 2010) a third were prepared to accept any (graduate) job they were offered, and a fifth admitted that they had applied to employers they weren't really interested in simply because they felt they didn't have much choice, given how tough the labour market was looking. The key thing for them was to secure a point of entry into the labour market.

brilliant example

'You can't expect to have it immediately – you might do a few jobs and then, suddenly, you know: oh, *this* is what I want to do. For me, it's important to keep your brain going. To keep learning something is always going to be better than doing nothing. And if you can't get the job you want, do any job. Earning some money is better than earning no money.'

Sophie, employee, Evotel Holdings

We've looked at transferable skills and how the skills, knowledge and understanding that you develop in one job stay with you. This means that you can evolve as a graduate worker, increasing your know-how and thereby increasing your value to an employer. It is also crucial to recognise that you can start your evolution from day one of an entry-level job. You'll then arrive at a point where you are ready to move on, to look for a greater challenge and a better paid job. This is what we call leverage in the job market.

Points of leverage

A longitudinal study tracked graduates not only into their first job on graduation (their point of entry – what is called the first destination in the national data collection), but also as they moved through the graduate labour market for several years further on. The researchers discovered that, three-and-a-half years after graduation, 81 per cent were in graduate occupations (that is, jobs for which a degree is required) and 87 per cent were 'fairly satisfied' or 'very satisfied' with their job. Leverage got them where they wanted to be. So, even if your point of entry is less than brilliant, you will find points of leverage towards your brilliant career.

 recap

- Graduates have proven thinking skills.

- They have shown that they are prepared to learn.

- They want to progress in their career and to develop their range of competencies (their professional repertoire).

- They can bring flexibility and innovation to an organisation.

- They bring skills, attitudes and behaviours which can enhance a company's productivity.

- Over half of the graduate jobs advertised don't specify the degree discipline: you can apply no matter what subject you study.

- Include small to medium-sized enterprises in your jobsearch.

- Develop transferable skills in everything you do: paid employment, voluntary work, daily life.

What to do next

A very simple next step would be to locate your own degree in Chapter 3 and read through what graduates have done overall, and what kind of occupational sectors they have gone for.

You could make a note of what interests you, and then follow it up by getting more information from your university careers service, or by using some of the other chapters in the first part of this handbook to move you on.

You could also look at the list of transferable skills and see if you can identify examples from your own experience which demonstrate you have that skill. This is as much a help for you yourself as it is for a potential employer. If there is an employability module on offer, have another look at it and see if it could help you – or if it did help you and you didn't realise it at the time.

CHAPTER 3

Labour market information: analysis of what graduates do

This chapter is in two sections. The first section takes you through labour market information, labour market intelligence and labour market experience. It explains what each of the terms mean, and how all of them can work together to support you in focusing your jobsearch.

The second section is much longer, because it takes you through what real graduates actually went on to do in the first six months after completing their first degree. You won't work through the whole of this section, just focus in on your own subject discipline to see what people who did the same degree as you went on to do in their careers.

SECTION ONE

What is labour market information (LMI)?

Confusingly enough, LMI can stand for two things, both of them important for any jobseeker which includes, of course, the graduate jobseeker. LMI can refer either to labour market information, or to labour market intelligence. Labour here means simply to do with work, and Market here describes the interactions between employers who need labour (or workers, to put it another way) and employees (those who can supply that labour or undertake that work). For graduates, LMI is collected by subject discipline. So you can look at what graduates from a particular discipline actually went on to do once they had graduated. This chapter works through the arguments for making use of LMI, and then looks in turn at what graduates from 27 different degree disciplines went on to do.

 **definition**

Labour market information means everything to do with employers and workers. This includes statistical information on vacancies, redundancies, people moving in and out of unemployment and people moving in and out of employment.

Why do you need to know about LMI?

This may all seem rather technical and you may well be wondering why you need to know anything at all about LMI when all you want to do is get started on your brilliant career. Well, the reason you need to know about LMI is because you live in a world that responds to the inevitable flux and changes within the labour market and particularly within the graduate labour market. If you are blissfully unaware that demand is changing you may well be trying to chase a kind of job that simply no longer exists. You might then start to think that this is all your fault, that you'll never find your way through the labour market. However, if you know that the market is changing, you know that you need to adapt to the new reality. Also, if you can be clear about what exactly the demand is for, you can tailor your jobsearch to the jobs that are actually on offer right now, rather than chasing jobs that exist only in your dreams or in the memories of others who haven't kept up with how the job market has changed since their day – which could mean only a few years rather than decades ago.

 **tip**

If you understand what is happening in the graduate labour market, you can be smarter in your jobsearch.

Points of entry and points of leverage in the labour market

The two concepts of knowing where jobs are and knowing when to move in or out of a job or sector are also key elements of moving into and through the job market. Moving in being the 'point of entry' and moving on being the 'point of leverage'. Knowing that you have amassed skills that are in demand and that therefore the time is right either to take any job now or to move on from that entry-level job is also important. Thus, understanding the labour market means that you are making informed decisions and that you have some sense of direction in the real world.

brilliant definitions

Point of **entry** means the first job you do to get into a particular area of the labour market. This could mean the graduate labour market, or the arts profession labour market or the labour market in Merseyside.

Point of **leverage** means that you have skills, knowledge, experience and know-how, which are in demand in the labour market, so you can use them to move from one job to another, or one occupational sector to another, normally to secure what you consider to be a better job.

Broaden your jobsearch horizons

Understanding the labour market can also help you to broaden your horizons: you will come across occupational sectors and jobs that you may not even have heard of, and you will see that people with a degree like yours have gone on to do a whole range of graduate jobs that you may never have considered. Thus, knowing what is happening in the job market will give you the courage to expand the range of jobs you are prepared to consider. It allows you to envisage yourself working in an occupational sector quite different from the one your original, limited outlook pointed you to. By keeping more options open, you increase your chances of securing graduate employment – even when more people are chasing fewer jobs. So now let's look at what you need to know to make sense of the labour market.

How LMI is collected

Quantitative and qualitative data

Labour market information simply means data collected on work; and includes data on job vacancies, employment, unemployment and employees. Labour market information can be either qualitative or quantitative.

Quantitative LMI is statistical and is often gathered by conducting a survey or taking a sample which is representative and can, therefore, reliably be generalised to offer conclusions. Quantitative LMI is often referred to as 'hard' data. It can be presented in spreadsheets or tables, or can be depicted as charts, graphs or maps.

Qualitative data are often gathered using research techniques such as focus groups or interviews, which can be in person or (in the case of interviews) done by phone. Qualitative data can be presented as case study or illustration. Filmed interviews of people talking about their experience of work can give you a powerful insight and real sense of immediacy (have a look at **www.careersbox.co.uk**). These approaches yield rich data, which can enhance our understanding of what the statistics seem to be telling us.

Geographical and sectoral territories

LMI is normally collected by territory. Territory can mean a geographical area, so LMI can be collected at a local, regional, national, European or even global level. Territory can also be defined by the kind of work that is done or by the kind of worker that does it, so we can collect statistical data by occupational sector, or by what kind of employers or by what kind of job. For these last two, there are agreed classifications so that comparisons can be easily made. The Employer classification is called the Standard Industrial Classification (SIC) and the Job classification is the Standard Occupational Classification (SOC).

Interrogating the data

Although it is tempting to take this kind of LMI at face value and trust it implicitly, the quality of the data can't be taken for granted and you need to be an intelligent consumer – more of which later. It can also be presented in reports that might be specialist by authorship (e.g. written by economists), specialist by readership (e.g. aimed at graduate jobseekers) or generalist (e.g. written by journalists and published in a newspaper for general readership).

Labour market intelligence

Labour market intelligence refers to the outcome of analysing labour market information, so it simply means taking the data (whether statistical, anecdotal or a combination of the two) and critically analysing them. Sometimes the data or the facts can simply 'speak for themselves' and there is no need to do anything more then present them, preferably in an accessible way. Other times it is helpful to look for what these data could be telling us: and so the analyst (or writer or presenter) tries to look for meaning in them. Obviously, meaning can be very subjective: the analysis might seek to present the data in the best possible light perhaps to encourage a slow job market, or to downplay emerging problems. We should also remember that statistics themselves are subjective: what is collected, from what sample population, at what time and for what purpose are just some of the parameters that are not given automatically but set for each individual survey or report. In fact, all labour market information and all labour market intelligence will have in it somewhere some element of subjectivity; so long as you are aware of this, you can approach LMI as an intelligent consumer, making your own mind up about what is presented to you, and deciding for yourself whether it is illuminating or helpful to you in your particular circumstances.

brilliant definition

Labour market intelligence consists of either quantitative or qualitative data, or a combination of the two. It is often presented as statistics, tables or graphs. It may also include some written analysis or commentary which explains what the data show.

Labour market experience

Sometimes, labour market information can be anecdotal, where one person recounts a particular experience (their own or that of someone else). This can also be referred to as labour market experience. Anecdotal information can be very helpful in giving us a way into the statistical data, or offering a picture of lived experience. Getting a sense of what a particular job feels like to someone who has done it can really enhance the statistical data, and give us a much fuller understanding of what the data tell us, which is why we have used case studies throughout the book and why we suggest you have a look at some online films where people talk about their own experience of jobs within occupational sectors. However, there is a danger in generalising from anecdotal information: of assuming that because one person had a bad experience of a job then everybody will have an equally bad experience of that job. To generalise from anecdotal information is inappropriate: we can generalise only from data that are robust enough to sustain that process.

 **definition**

> **Labour market experience** draws on the individual story. It offers powerful insight into what it feels like to do a given job, but can't be used for generalisation.

How to be an intelligent consumer of LMI

Part of your training as a graduate is to challenge what is taken for granted, to inquire and to reach your own conclusions. This applies equally to how you should approach LMI. There are a few key tests that you should run through when you come across labour market information in whatever form it is presented to you. Whether that's information from an employer, a newspaper report on what's happening to graduates in the job market, or what someone you know says about unemployment, job opportunities or transferable skills. The three key tests are for: currency, validity and fitness for purpose.

Currency: how up to date is the information?

If written or published, even if the article is pretty fresh, is there a date given for the data set that has been used as the base for the article? If someone is talking about an experience, how far back does it go? And how old do you think things have to be before they are questionable in their relevance to the here and now? Have things in the sector you are looking at changed much over the last few years or stayed pretty stable? Do you have a feel for the currency of the data: is it past its sell-by date or still fit for consumption? Although you need to go back several years (even decades) to identify a trend and, although there is, inevitably, a time lag between data collection and its publication, we wouldn't expect information to be much more than a couple of years old.

Validity: how reliable is the information?

Is the source reliable – and do you actually know what the source of the information is? If it is in print, does the article quote or refer to the source of the original data? If online, can you identify who either the author or the source is? Could there be any advantage for them in presenting a particular perspective – perhaps to back up a point they want to make or to present something in a good light? Could there be any 'spin' on this? Look at any footnotes – check if they explain any rounding up of figures or acknowledge that things have been left out. Omissions can be perfectly legitimate and even necessary (for example, when a sample size is too small to be of statistical significance), but this should be made clear. Is there any sense of presenting competing perspectives or alternative interpretations, or is the commentary rather fixed in its views?

Is the LMI fit for purpose?

Does the information or article tell you something you need to know? Is it helpful to you in getting you to think afresh? Perhaps it has helped you to examine what you yourself have taken for granted or assumed to be the case without really knowing what the basis for your assumptions is and therefore your own take on the issue. Look at the sample size and the composition of the sample: does it make sense to you? Ultimately, the question here is whether the LMI is relevant to you and what you are trying to do in the labour market. It may not seem immediately relevant; you may have to run these quick tests to work out if it helps you, or not.

 **tip**

Intelligent consumers check labour market information by asking these questions before taking action.

- **Currency**   Is this information sufficiently up to date?
- **Validity**   Is it reliable: is the source noted somewhere?
- **Relevance**   Is it telling me anything new or something I need to know?

It doesn't matter in what order you apply the tests and, to some extent, it doesn't even matter how rigorously you apply them. What matters is that you consider the LMI in front of you, you do your best to make sense of it, you interrogate your superficial impressions and you make an informed decision whether or not to take this particular nugget of LMI into account as you navigate your way into or around the graduate labour market.

How do we know what graduates actually do on completion of their degree?

Destinations of Leavers from Higher Education Institutions (DLHE)

One source of LMI passes all three of the key tests outlined here and we are going to make extensive use of it in this chapter. It is the annual *DLHE* report or, to give it its full title, *Destinations of Leavers from Higher Education Institutions*. The Higher Education Statistics Agency (HESA) collects information on what graduates are doing six months after completion of an undergraduate or foundation degree. First destinations cover: employment; training; further study, or a combination of these. They also include: working overseas; not being available for employment; being unemployed or presumed to be unemployed.

Who is included in the data collection?

Data are collected from students who are domiciled in the UK and the EU: they don't include overseas students who are not normally resident in the UK. Students are invited to respond, via questionnaire, in the winter following the summer in which they graduated, which means that someone who graduated in Summer 2009 responds in December 2009. The destination data are published the following summer; so the responses of the class of 2009 are published as raw data in July 2010. The Higher Education Careers Services Unit (HECSU) and the Education Liaison Task Group of the Association of Graduate Careers Advisory Services (AGCAS) then work together to write *What do graduates do? (WDGD)* This is published annually in November. The most recent edition of *WDGD*, which uses data from those who graduated in the summer of 2009, was published in November 2010: this is the edition we have used.

What kind of jobs do graduates do?

Where students report that they are in employment, they are asked to give some more detail on the kind of job they are doing and the kind of employer they are working for. This allows the data to be classified for easy comparison across occupation and across sector. The *DLHE* data and the *WDGD* report give us a pretty accurate snapshot of what graduates go into as their first destination.

brilliant tip

Look at what other graduates with your degree have gone on to do and note where they have moved into an occupational sector that might seem far removed from the subject area you are studying. Remember that you are developing thinking, competence and transferable skills, so you can move around the labour market. Widening your jobsearch increases the number of jobs you can consider, thus increasing your chance of securing graduate employment.

Increase the sample size by completing your own DLHE *data request*

It is worth adding here that, the more respondents there are, the more comprehensive the sample set is. So if you are reading this as a final-year undergraduate, please respond to the questionnaire when you receive it a few months after your own graduation.

Not every degree subject is included in WDGD

WDGD is certainly pretty comprehensive in its coverage of undergraduate degrees. Some degree titles are grouped into a broader discipline category, for example Women's Studies is included in Sociology, and War Studies is included in History. For foundation degrees, there is no distinction by discipline; rather the analysis is of the whole cohort of students who completed their Foundation degree in that year, irrespective of the subject they studied. Data for biomedical degrees (Medicine, Nursing, Anatomy, Physiology and Pathology, Pharmacology, Toxicology and Pharmacy, Occupational Therapy, Physiotherapy and Teaching degrees) are published separately and can be accessed on the Graduate Prospects website (**www.prospects.ac.uk**).

Limitations of the DLHE *survey*

Although the destination data are very useful, the first destination survey does have its limitations. For example, we don't know *why* graduates choose these particular paths or went into these particular jobs. Nor do we know how long they are going to stay in their first destination. A graduate can be working in a bar every night, whilst making applications and going for job interviews all day, every day. Overnight, their employment status changes category: from 'Retail, catering, waiting and bar staff' to ' Social and welfare professionals', but their first destination on graduating will, forever, be bar work. Also, in a sense, the report is backward looking: it tells us what has happened, but can't forecast how things might be in the future. Obviously, we can identify changes and, if those changes are consistent over a few years, we can even identify trends, which helps us make sense of what has happened, and can alert us to things changing in the future. But the *DLHE* survey doesn't pretend to be anything more than a clear snapshot of the first destination of UK domiciled students six months after they graduate.

Ensure you access current data

Although general trends are not likely to change significantly year on year, it is nevertheless important to check for currency. As there is inevitably a time lag between data collection and their analysis, publications can become dated and are regularly superseded. Online sources are more easily updated than printed versions, so do follow the leads below if you want to be sure you are up to the minute.

Graduate Prospects

This is the best point of reference for graduates, because that is what it specialises in and is set up to do. It addresses final-year undergraduates in particular, so don't just bookmark it – consult it.

UK Commission for Employment and Skills

Signposts expert and up-to-date articles on sector changes and general trends including, but not limited to, graduate entry.

Office for National Statistics (ONS)

Publishes a wide range of official statistics for the United Kingdom, including reports on the labour market in general, not just the graduate labour market. It also produces a regular bulletin called *Intelligence*. This includes analytical comment including, but not restricted to, the labour market. You can sign up for alerts when the latest edition is published.

Annual Survey of Hours and Earnings (ASHE)

This is also published by ONS. It gives overall population and trend data, which is helpful when you want to put graduate information in context against the wider, more general, labour market.

 **recap**

- LMI can mean labour market information, i.e. data.

- LMI can mean labour market intelligence, i.e. data plus analysis.

- Labour market experience reflects lived experience of a particular job, and it can illuminate what the data tell us.

- Use your critical faculties when you come across LMI.

- Look at your own degree subject as well as some others.

- Point of entry means your first graduate job.

- Point of leverage is job changing once you have competencies.

SECTION 2

What do graduates do?

The next part follows the sequence used by *WDGD*, which comprises six broad categories of undergraduate study, plus all Foundation degree subjects. The groupings are as follows:

1 Science (Biology; Chemistry; Environmental Science; Physics; and Sports Science).

2 Mathematics, IT and Computing.

3 Engineering and Building Management (Architecture and Building; Civil Engineering; Electrical and Electronic Engineering; and Mechanical Engineering).

4 Social Sciences (Economics, Geography, Law, Politics, Psychology; and Sociology).

5 Arts, Creative Arts and Humanities (Art and Design; English; History; Media Studies; Languages; and Performing Arts).

6 Business and Administrative Studies (Accountancy; Business and Management; and Marketing).

7 Foundation degrees (all subjects studied at this level).

These broad categories are then broken down into degree subject. For example, Science comprises: Biology; Chemistry; Environmental; Physical Geographical & Terrestrial Sciences; Physics; and finally Sports Science. These headings in turn embrace quite a range of specialisms in congruent areas of study. Chemistry, for example, lists Inorganic Chemistry, Petrochemical Chemistry and Crystallography, to name but 3 of the 21 titles included.

For every degree subject, we start by setting out the *Range* of degree courses included. For some, the range of degrees is relatively limited, e.g. Accountancy. For others, the range is considerable, e.g. Performing Arts. For most subjects, it is really interesting to see the multiple perspectives that are possible within an over-arching subject area.

We then go on to report on the *Response rate and destination percentages*, so you can see how many students actually responded and, of these, what percentages went into employment, combined work and study, or went on to study in the UK or overseas. The categories also include people who were not available for study (perhaps through illness) and the percentage of graduates unemployed at that point in time. We always present these in the same order for ease of comparison. We have left out the percentages of graduates going into 'other occupations' and 'unknown occupations' because we want to share with you what we know about what graduates have actually gone on to do. This means that sometimes the figures provided will not add up to 100 per cent, but that doesn't affect the overall picture of what occupational areas graduates go for.

Finally, we look at *What occupational sectors did they go for?* where we drill into what kind of employment respondents from that discipline went on to do. This gives you a sense of what jobs were taken up, and what employers were recruiting. There are only a handful of examples for a response size of thousands, but it does help to illustrate the statistical data. Please note that, where necessary, we have followed the convention of rounding percentages up or down to one decimal point, because it makes the numbers a little easier to read. This means that sometimes the totals (for example, of the destination percentages) are slightly more or less than 100 per cent. Obviously, this doesn't alter the overall picture of what graduates do.

In a handful of cases, the total number of respondents is greater than the sum of female and male respondents. This can happen where someone sends a response, but doesn't specify their gender. Obviously, it is important to include such responses in the sample, although that does throw up this anomaly.

How to use this section

You can use this section to see what other people, doing the same kind of degree as you have gone on to do. This can reassure you that you are not on your own in your chosen field. Or it can challenge and inspire you to think more widely in your jobsearch. It can also help you to counteract some of the uninformed advice (no doubt well-intentioned) that may be putting you off track. The most important benefit of this section is that you will end up better informed about labour market information in relation to your current field of study.

brilliant dos and don'ts

Do

✔ check out what people on your degree course have actually gone on to do;

✔ think about broadening your jobsearch to include jobs you haven't thought about or maybe hadn't heard of before;

✔ think about points of entry and then points of leverage.

Don't

✘ rely on what other people remember from their day: things change, particularly in labour markets;

✘ worry that your job isn't a graduate or professional job; you can learn a great deal and use that for leverage;

✘ despair at gloomy headlines: graduates are still in demand and are still being employed, even if it takes time and effort.

1 Science

Five subject areas are included within Science, namely: Biology; Chemistry; Environmental Science; Physics and Sports Science. Biology has more female than male students with Physics the reverse: here males outnumber females by nearly 5:1. Sports Science is by far the biggest by student numbers. Physics, by contrast, is the smallest by student number. Sports Science also has the highest proportion of students going into employment, and Physics the highest proportion of students going on to higher degrees.

▶ brilliant example

'I completed my undergraduate degree in Sport and Exercise Sciences. The department put a strong emphasis on how the theory we are taught can be and currently is being used within applied settings, by actively encouraging students to get their "hands dirty" and get out into the applied setting to get as much applied experience as possible. Several internships and placements were on offer for willing students to get involved in. I'm now employed as a performance analyst at a county cricket club and am enjoying working within one of my favoured sports, and learning how performance analysis is perceived and used within cricket. I think that my placements at Warrington, Liverpool FC and Stoke City FC and the skills and experience I have gained made my CV stand out. I would advise students to follow the advice I was given and get their "hands dirty" in as much applied experience as possible.'

Stuart, BSc (Hons) Sport and Exercise Sciences

1.1 Biology

Range

Biology degrees include specialisms within the discipline, such as Cell, Reproductive, Population Biology and Biometry. There are specialisms by context such as Freshwater, Marine Biology and Parasitology. Applied Biology, of course, and also Applied Cell Biology. Biodiversity and Ecology are also here.

Response rate and destination percentages

A total of 3,460 graduates responded, 84.1% of graduates in these disciplines. There were 2,100 female and 1,355 male respondents. 45% of these graduates were in UK employment, with a further 1.5% in overseas employment. 7.3% were combining work with studying. Added together, that makes 54.8% in employment. 17.6% went on to study in the UK for a higher degree, which included PhD Stem Cell Biology, MSc Medical and Nuclear Microbiology and MSc Forensic Science. 4.9% progressed to the Postgraduate Certificate of Education (PGCE), with another 4.9% taking on other further study in the UK. 0.4% undertook further study overseas, bringing the total percentage of students studying to 27.8%, which is rather higher than the average across all degree disciplines. 3.9% were unavailable for employment, study or training, 4.3% came into the 'other' category, leaving 10% reporting unemployed.

What occupational sectors did they go for?

12.1% of employed graduates secured work in scientific research, analysis and development professionals, including jobs such as a healthcare scientist in the NHS and a food microbiologist for a leading confectionery company. Of course, many scientific research jobs will demand a higher degree, which is, in part, why a higher proportion of Biology students progress to higher education compared with all graduates. A further 12% went into other professional jobs, including political researcher for the Foreign Office. Health professional jobs account for 4.7% of these graduates, and education professionals for another 4.6%, jobs here including Science teachers. Business and finance professionals absorbed 3.9% and included trainee accountant with Ernst & Young. 9% went into clerical and secretarial occupations, and 15.8% into other occupations. Retail, catering, waiting and bar staff took 20.5% of employed graduates but the degree discipline is evident in employment such as scientific sales assistant.

1.2 Chemistry

Range

The range of Chemistry degrees reflects orientation within the discipline, including: Analytical; Biomolecular; Polymer; Structural; and Organic

Chemistry. Degree title can also reflect application and/or sector, such as: Pharmaceutical; Petrochemical; Medicinal; Industrial and Colour Chemistry.

Response rate and destination percentages

A total of 2,270 graduates responded, 85.5% of graduates in these disciplines. There were 900 female and 1,280 male respondents. 39.4% of these graduates were in UK employment, with a further 1.2% in overseas employment. 5.5% were combining work with studying. Added together, that makes 46.1% in employment. 29.8% went on to study in the UK for a higher degree, which included PhD Chemical Biology and MSc Imaging in Biomedical Research. 5.3% progressed to PGCE, with 2.9% taking on other further study in the UK, including the graduate diploma in Law. 0.4% undertook further study overseas, bringing the studying total to 38.5%. 3.3% were unavailable for employment, study or training, 3.4% came into the 'other' category, leaving 8.7% reporting unemployed.

What occupational sectors did they go for?

Roughly equal percentages of these Chemistry graduates went into two professional domains: 17.1% are classified as scientific, research, analysis and development professionals, and 18.4% as other professional and technical. The scientific professional jobs included technologist for Cadbury and gold consultant for a jeweller. Then follows a tail of professional destinations: business and finance professionals claimed 8.5%, education professionals 4.4%, marketing, sales and administration took 3.2%, engineering professionals 2.3%, health and associate professionals 1.7%. 13.4% went into retail, catering, waiting and bar staff, with jobs here including buyer for Sainsbury's and retail manager for Debenhams. Management jobs in commercial and public services accounted for 7.4%. Other occupations, which includes officer cadet in the British Army, absorb 11.7%.

1.3 Environmental, Physical Geographical and Terrestrial Sciences

Range

This section encompasses an interesting range of related scientific disciplines including: Physical and Maritime Geography, Geomorphology,

Cartography and Geographical Information Systems, Meteorology, Climatology and Pollution Control.

Response rate and destination percentages

A total of 2,260 graduates responded, 85.8% of graduates in these disciplines. There were 1,315 female and 1,340 male respondents. 50.4% of these graduates were in UK employment, with a further 2.1% in overseas employment. 6.6% were combining work with studying. Added together, that makes 59.1% in employment. 15.6% went on to study in the UK for a higher degree, which included PhD Quaternary Research, MSc Environmental Modelling and MA Creative Cities. 4.9% progressed to PGCE, with 2.6% taking on other further study in the UK. With 0.2% studying overseas, the studying total is 23.6%. 5.5% were unavailable for employment, study or training, 3.5% came into the 'other' category, leaving 8.3% reporting unemployed.

What occupational sectors did they go for?

The biggest single destination was retail, catering, waiting and bar staff with 24.9% of all employed graduates from these disciplines. Other occupations accounted for a further 16.3% and other clerical occupations for 11.2%. The professional destinations did show the relevance of the discipline. 8.8% went into other professions, with jobs including assistant coastal engineer for a local authority. Scientific professionals absorbed only 1.8% but included climate research officer for the Shetland Islands Council. Engineering professionals was of similar significance with only 1.6%. 7.7% secured professional jobs in business and finance, including trainee accountant for KPMG and accounts executive for Barclays. A significant sector here is commercial and public sector managers, which accounted for 12.4% of the employed graduates.

1.4 Physics

Range

With very few exceptions (Acoustics, Electromagnetism and Quantum Mechanics) the degrees included here have Physics firmly in the title: Maths and Theoretical Physics, Quantum and Computational Physics.

The descriptor may well relate to the orientation by sector: Engineering, Chemical, Medical, Optical and Environmental Physics, for example.

Response rate and destination percentages

A total of 1,895 graduates responded, 86.9% of graduates in these disciplines. There were 395 female and 1,500 male respondents, putting the gender balance firmly with male students. 31.3% of these graduates were in UK employment, with a further 1.8% in overseas employment. 6.8% were combining work with studying. Added together, that makes 39.9% in employment. Overall, a higher proportion of students went on to study: 40.4% in all. This breaks down into an impressive 33.2% progressing to higher degrees in the UK including PhD Astrophysics, MSc Sustainable Energy Systems and in Photon Science. 4% progressed to PGCE, another 2.3% taking on other further study in the UK, and 0.9% studying overseas. The 40% study rate is much higher than the average of 15.4% across all first degree subjects. 4.5% were unavailable for employment, study or training, 3.5% came into the 'other' category, leaving 11.7% believed to be unemployed.

What occupational sectors did they go for?

In terms of professional destinations, business and finance takes the greatest percentage, with 15.8%. Jobs here include trainee auditor with KPMG and supply chain planner for Rolls Royce. Scientific and engineering professions absorb 8.6% and 8.2% respectively, and include research scientist and optics engineer. Information technology and education professions take 6.8% and 6.5% respectively, with marketing, sales and advertising professionals and arts, design, culture and sports professionals also well matched at 2.9% and 2.8% respectively. Commercial and public service managers claimed 7.5% and included project manager with Network Rail. In common with many other disciplines, retail, catering, waiting and bar staff was a significant destination at 11.6%.

1.5 Sports Science

Range

The range in Sports Science is not wide. It includes Exercise Science, Science in Health, Exercise and Sport and then a cluster of titles which indicate the application in practice: Conditioning, Development, Therapy and Rehabilitation.

Response rate and destination percentages

This is the biggest student body within the Science division, with a total of 6,110 graduates responding, 82.3% of graduates in these disciplines. There were 2,475 female and 3,635 male respondents. 59.6% of these graduates were in UK employment, with a further 1.3% in overseas employment. 8.5% were combining work with studying. Added together, that makes an impressive 69.4% in employment. 6% went on to study in the UK for a higher degree, which included MSc Applied Sport and MSc Public Health and Health Promotion. 6% progressed to PGCE, with 3.4% taking on other further study in the UK. With only 0.2% studying overseas, the studying total is 15.6%. 4.2% were unavailable for employment, study or training, 3.7% came into the 'other' category, leaving 6.9% reporting unemployed.

What occupational sectors did they go for?

The biggest single destination, at 21.1%, was arts, design, culture and sports professions, jobs here including rugby coach with a local council and strength and conditioning coach with London Irish RFU. A similar proportion (21.3%) fall into other occupations. 11.1% went into education professions, with jobs such as sports development officer for a local council. With social and welfare accounting for a further 5.2%, there then follows a flurry of small percentages: 2.8% to health professions, 2.7% to business and finance professions, 2.5% to marketing, sales and advertising professions and 1.8% to other professions. Although still modest, a larger percentage (7.6%) went into commercial and public service management, including club manager with Total Fitness. 15.7% went into retail, catering, waiting and bar work, including retail management with Marks & Spencer.

2 Mathematics, IT and Computing

There are two subject areas included in this short section. Mathematics stands alone, followed by Computer Science and IT. Both disciplines have more male than female students. In Maths the male to female ratio is not that much, certainly less than 2:1. But in Computer Science and IT the difference is very noticeable, nearer 5:1. For Maths students, the percentage going on to higher study is well above average. Although there have been some surprising falls in employment rates, particularly for Computing graduates, their numeracy and other transferable skills give them scope in the labour market.

▶ brilliant example

'Maths is my passion: I really enjoyed my course, which taught me so much. I was also able to develop many other useful skills during my studies including communication, time management and organisation. As part of my course I got involved in a recycling project at a housing trust. I gained a lot of experience about the environment and associated issues. It also gave me an insight into full-time working and the pressures that go with it. I successfully gained a job working as a research assistant for an innovations company, which I really enjoy.'

Jo, BSc (Hons) Mathematics

2.1 Mathematics

Range

The range of degrees included is narrow. It includes Pure, Applied, Engineering and Industrial Mathematics, Mathematical Modelling, Numerical Method and Numerical Analysis.

Response rate and destination percentages

A total of 3,865 graduates responded, 84.1% of graduates in these disciplines. There were 1,615 female and 2,250 male respondents. 40.4% of these graduates were in UK employment, with a further 1.2% in overseas employment. 12.1% were combining work with studying. Added together, that makes 53.7% in employment. 14.8% went on to study in the UK for a higher degree, which included PhD Statistics, MPhil Mathematics, MSc Medical Statistics, MSc Information Systems and MMus in Musicology. 8.4% progressed to PGCE, with 3.8% taking on other further study in the UK and 0.3% studying overseas, bringing the studying total to 27.3%. 4.5% were unavailable for employment, study or training, 4.2% came into the 'other' category, leaving 10.3% reporting unemployed.

What occupational sectors did they go for?

The majority destination, with 33%, is business and financial professionals, where the numeracy of the degree discipline is directly relevant. Jobs here included actuary with the Prudential, assistant accountant with KPMG and finance auditor with Deloitte. Other professional destinations follow behind: 9.5% into education professions, not just as Maths teacher but also English Language teaching abroad. 5.6% into IT professional jobs, including software engineer and analyst. Marketing, sales and advertising professionals took 2.3%, with smaller percentages going into engineering and scientific professions: 1.3% and 1.4% respectively. In total, over 53% of jobs were in professional categories. In addition, 7% went into commercial or public service management. Retail, catering, waiting and bar staff absorbed 12.9% and included jobs such as merchandiser for Tesco and business analyst for Marks and Spencer. 9% went into other clerical, 4.9% into numerical clerks and cashiers, and 7.2% into the other occupations category.

2.2 Computer Science and IT

Range

A wide range of degree titles is included in the broad category of Computer Science and IT. It includes Computer Science, Computer Vision and Computer Architecture. There is a cluster around programming including Procedural and Declarative Programming. Systems Analysis is here, along with Systems Design and Systems Auditing. The final sub-set would include Artificial Intelligence, Speech and Language Processing, and Neural Computing.

Response rate and destination percentages

A total of 8,995 graduates responded, 80.6% of graduates in the discipline. There were 1,545 female and 7,455 male respondents, making these male-dominated subjects. 57.4% of these graduates were in UK employment, with a further 1% in overseas employment. 5.5% were combining work with studying. Added together, that makes 63.9% in employment. 7.5% went on to study in the UK for a higher degree, which included PhD Computer Science, MPhil Mobile Computing, MSc Web Development, Computer Animation and Entrepreneurship, and the specialist Masters in Business Administration (MBA). 1.2% progressed to PGCE, with 2.5% taking on other further study in the UK and 0.1% studying overseas, bringing the studying total to 11.3%. 2.6% were unavailable for employment, study or training, 5.7% came into the 'other' category, leaving 16.3% reporting unemployed.

What occupational sectors did they go for?

Most of the graduates who secured employment got jobs as information technology professionals: a pleasing 38.9%. The job titles reflect the degree titles mentioned earlier, and include: IT manager, IT officer and IT consultant with HM Government, a higher education institution and the BBC respectively. Jobs as telecoms engineer with O_2 and software engineer with Xerox again reflect the focus of undergraduate study. There then follows quite a long tail of other professional sectors: 6.1% into arts, design, culture and sports professionals; 4.8% into business and finance professionals, with jobs such as data analyst for Barclays Capital and resource analyst for Barclaycard. Education professionals account for 2.8%, marketing and sales professionals for another 2.4%, engineering professionals for 1.7%. There was a greater percentage going into commercial and public service management at 9.2%. A similar percentage, 9.5%, went into other occupations. 6.1% went into clerical and secretarial work. A significant percentage, some 13.7%, went into retail, catering, waiting and bar staff, including a graduate traineeship in personnel with Tesco. This should not obscure the fact that 56.7% of these graduates went into professional jobs, a total rising to almost 66% when management destinations are included.

3 Engineering and Building Management

There are four subject areas included here: Architecture and Building, Civil Engineering, Electrical and Electronic Engineering and Mechanical

Engineering. Men outnumber women across the board, although the ratio varies, from roughly 2:1 in Architecture and Building, through 6:1 in Civil Engineering to 11:1 in Mechanical Engineering. Employment rates in each of the disciplines is higher than the average across all graduates from all subjects. It is highest in Civil Engineering. Closer scrutiny of the destination data shows high proportions of graduates secure work as professionals in their field. This may be only to be expected, but should nonetheless be celebrated.

brilliant example

'From around my GSCEs onwards, I thought that I would enjoy a career in Civil Engineering. It seemed suited to my skills in Maths and Physics, particularly Mechanics, and Physical Geography. During my second year studying Civil Engineering I started to realise I had doubts about whether Civil Engineering would be right for me. I wondered if it might be possible to transfer . . . to another part of the engineering industry, one that had interested me for a long time: motorsport. I realised I would need a more relevant degree to appeal to potential employers (in motorsport). I also thought it crucial to finish my Masters in Civil Engineering . . . in case I needed to fall back on it, as this is a well-respected degree throughout the engineering sector. I'm now a systems engineer on a Formula One team.'

Oliver, MEng Civil Engineering, MSc Motorsport Engineering and Management

3.1 Architecture and Building

Range

Architecture degrees are here, of course: Architectural Design Theory and Architectural Technology. Building degrees too: Construction Management, Building Technology and Conservation of Buildings. Closely related is Surveying, with both Building and Quantity Surveying. Landscape is evident in Landscape Architecture, Studies and Design and a wider perspective brings in Planning, ranging from Regional, Rural and Urban to Housing and Transport Planning.

Response rate and destination percentages

A total of 5,980 graduates responded, 82.1% of graduates in these disciplines. There were 1,635 female and 4,345 male respondents. 58.5% of these graduates were in UK employment, with a further 1.6% in overseas employment. 7.9% were combining work with studying. Added together, that makes 68% in employment. 6.3% went on to study in the UK for a higher degree, which included MA in Architecture, MSc Property Management and Development and the Graduate Diploma in Building Surveying. 0.2% progressed to PGCE, with 6.4% taking on other further study in the UK and 0.1% studying overseas, bringing the studying total to 13%. 3.7% were unavailable for employment, study or training, 4.5% came into the 'other' category, leaving 10.9% reporting unemployed.

What occupational sectors did they go for?

A very high proportion, 50.6%, went into the category of 'other professionals', which includes architectural assistant, architectural technician, trainee architect and quantity surveyor. It makes absolute sense that the vast majority of employment is secured here. Employers include private architectural firms and public service providers. Commercial and public service managers accounted for a further 12.5% with jobs such as construction manager and project manager for the NHS. 4% went into engineering professions, working as graduate and civil engineers for employers including Anglian Water. There follows a long tail of small percentages going into a range of sectors, with only 3.1% into business and finance, and 9.2% into retail, catering, waiting and bar staff.

3.2 Civil Engineering

Range

Civil Engineering covers a wider range of degrees than might be expected. Civil and Structural Engineering degrees, of course, plus Surveying degrees including Engineering Surveying and Surveying Science. Transport Engineering, Urban Studies and Permanent Way Engineering are joined by Environmental Engineering, Energy Resources, Environmental Impact and Coastal Decay.

Response rate and destination percentages

A total of 2,060 graduates responded, 84.3% of graduates in these disciplines. There were 295 female and 1,765 male respondents. 58.6% of these graduates were in UK employment, with a further 2% in overseas employment. 7.1% were combining work with studying. Added together, that makes 67.7% in employment. 10% went on to study in the UK for a higher degree, which included PhD in Civil Engineering, MPhil in Civil Engineering and MScs in Civil Engineering and Civil Engineering with Structural Engineering. 0.6% progressed to PGCE, with only 1.5% taking on other further study in the UK. With nobody studying overseas, the studying total is 12.1%. 5.3% were unavailable for employment, study or training, 2.9% came into the 'other' category, leaving 11.9% reporting unemployed.

What occupational sectors did they go for?

An impressive 58.2% of graduates employed went into engineering professions with job titles including civil, site, structural and geotechnical engineer. Employers included Mott MacDonald, Jacobs, Atkins and Network Rail. A further 11.3% entered other professions including quantity surveyor and trainee environment agency officer. There was a long tail of named professional sectors (e.g. health, education), but in total over 76% of graduates from civil engineering went into professional destinations. Commercial and public service management took 7.4% with jobs such as management trainee for a building contractor. This means that 83.5% of the graduates from these disciplines who entered employment went into professional or managerial jobs. That leaves a few smaller destinations: 7.6% into retail, catering, waiting and bar staff and 6.4% into 'other occupations'.

3.3 Electrical and Electronic Engineering

Range

The range is not very broad, including Electrical, Electrical Power, Electrical Power Generation and Electrical Power Distribution. Another cluster is degrees in Satellite, Telecommunications, Broadcast and Communications Engineering. Cybernetics, Robotics and Virtual Reality complete the list here.

Response rate and destination percentages

A total of 2,200 graduates responded, 82.4% of graduates in these disciplines. There were 205 female and 1,995 male respondents. 56.6% of these graduates were in UK employment, with a further 1.1% in overseas employment. 6% were combining work with studying. Added together, that makes 63.7% in employment. 12.7% went on to study in the UK for a higher degree, which included PhD in Electronic Engineering, MSc in Robotics and in Project Management. 1% progressed to PGCE, with 2% taking on other further study in the UK and 0.1% studying overseas. The total percentage of graduates studying is 15.8%. 2.6% were unavailable for employment, study or training, 4.6% came into the 'other' category, leaving 13.3% reporting unemployed.

What occupational sectors did they go for?

Engineering professionals is the majority destination, with 28.4% working as systems, flight systems, robotics, software or weapons engineers with employers such as BAE Systems, Ericsson and the Royal Navy. IT professions absorbed a further 18.5%, with jobs including website developer. 7.5% went into management in the commercial or public sector, working, for example, as a project manager with a data storage provider. It is interesting to note that a similar proportion, 7.7%, came under arts, design, culture and sports professionals. Business and finance professions took 2.9% in roles such as chartered accountant, and pricing analyst for Europcar. 12.4% went into retail, catering, waiting and bar staff, with 10.2% going into 'other occupations'.

3.4 Mechanical Engineering

Range

A range of specialism and sector is reflected in the degree titles included here: Road Vehicle, Automotive or Automobile Engineering; Rail Vehicle, Ship Propulsion, Marine and Offshore Engineering, Vibration, Acoustics, Fluid and, finally, Farm and Agriculture Engineering.

Response rate and destination percentages

A total of 2,430 graduates responded, 85.9% of graduates in these disciplines. There were 175 female and 2,255 male respondents, making

Mechanical Engineering the most male-dominated of all the degree disciplines studied. 58.1% of these graduates were in UK employment, with a further 2.4% in overseas employment. 5% were combining work with studying. Added together, that makes 65.5% in employment. 11.7% went on to study in the UK for a higher degree, which included MPhil Biomedical Engineering, MSc Renewable Energy and Engineering Management. 0.4% progressed to PGCE, with only 1.6% taking on other further study in the UK and 0.2% studying overseas. The total percentage of graduates studying is 13.9%. 5.1% were unavailable for employment, study or training, 3.8% came into the 'other' category, leaving 11.8% reporting unemployed.

What occupational sectors did they go for?

A very high proportion of these graduates (55.6%) secured engineering profession jobs with employers such as: Airbus, Mercedes-Benz, E.ON Central Networks and a Formula One team. 3.8% went into business and finance professions, including trainee broker and assistant auditor with employers including PricewaterhouseCoopers. A further 7.6% opted for commercial and public sector management. There was a small tail of other professions at 4.7% and IT professionals at 1.2%. In total 71% of these graduates secured professional jobs. Including managerial jobs this brings the total to 78.6.%, impressively high and just behind Civil Engineering on this count.

4 Social Sciences

Social Sciences comprises six disciplines: Economics; Geography; Law; Politics; Psychology; and Sociology. Only Economics and Politics have more male than female graduates and this is most pronounced in Economics, where males outnumber females by roughly 3:1. The other four subjects all have a majority of female students. This is roughly 2:1 in Law, 3:1 in Sociology and over 4:1 in Psychology. Law has a very high proportion (nearly 39%) of students going on to further study on graduation, more than double the average across all degree disciplines. This is readily explained by the need for further study for admission to the legal professions, including barrister and solicitor.

▶ brilliant example

'Originally I had chosen to study Psychology with Counselling Skills as a time-filler. It was meant to be a hobby only, or, at the very most, something which would improve my knowledge, giving me a head-start when it came to becoming a counsellor. Instead it changed my view of psychology and counselling quite dramatically. This changed my career path from becoming a counsellor to a health psychologist. Now working as a health promotion specialist . . . I am able to take the lead on many areas and have a huge amount of independence. The job is quite special in that way.'

Christopher, BA (Hons) Psychology with Counselling Skills

4.1 Economics

Range

The range of degrees included as Economics is pretty restricted, and simply reflects the various aspects of the discipline: Microeconomics, Macroeconomics, Econometrics, Capitalism, Keynesianism, Monetarism. It also includes topic-related degree names: Political, Financial, International or Agricultural Economics.

Response rate and destination percentages

A total of 3,485 graduates responded, 82.3% of graduates in these disciplines. There were 975 female and 2,510 male respondents, making Economics one of only two degree disciplines within the Social Sciences where men outnumber women (the other being Politics). 47.1% of these graduates were in UK employment, with a further 2% in overseas employment. 10.8% were combining work with studying. Added together, that makes 59.9% in employment. 14.4% went on to study in the UK for a higher degree, which included MSc Econometrics and, in Banking and International Finance, MA in Economics and in Risk Management. 0.8% progressed to PGCE, with 3.5% taking on other further study in the UK and 0.5% studying overseas. The total percentage of graduates studying was 19.2%. 5.8% were unavailable for employment, study or training, 4.1% came into the 'other' category, leaving 11% reporting unemployed.

What occupational sectors did they go for?

A significant proportion of economics graduates, 39.3%, secured employment as business and financial professionals, working variously as accountant or assistant auditor with employers such as Deloitte, Ernst & Young and KPMG. A smaller proportion was found in marketing sales and advertising professionals, some 5.2% employed here, for example, as marketing executive or account manager with employers including Thomson Reuters. 3% secured professional jobs within the catch-all 'other professions', including trainee recruitment consultant. Turning towards commercial and public sector managers, 13.4% found work, for example, as civil servant in the Welsh Government and intern in the Department of Business Innovation and Skills. 7.6% went into other clerical jobs, 6.2% into numerical clerks and cashiers, and 11.9% into retail, catering, waiting and bar staff.

4.2 Geography

Range

Geography degrees include Human and Social Geography, plus study by area, e.g. Europe, Australasia, Africa or the Americas. Study of Geography by topic includes Cultural, Historical, Political, Transport and Urban.

Response rate and destination percentages

A total of 2,085 graduates responded, 85.8% of all graduates in this category. As with most of the discipline in Social Sciences, there were more female respondents than male respondents, but with 1,195 female and 890 male respondents, this makes Geography a more balanced discipline in terms of female:male participation rates. 48.7% of these graduates were in UK employment, with a further 2.1% in overseas employment. 8% were combining work with studying. Added together, that makes 58.8% in employment. 15.4% went on to study in the UK for a higher degree, which included Masters in Town Planning, Meteorology and Climatology and Museum and Heritage. 4.9% went on to further study in the UK including the graduate diploma in Law, and 4.5%

progressed to PGCE. 0.2% were studying overseas, bringing the studying total to 25%. 5.4% were unavailable for employment, study or training. 3.5% came into the 'other' category, leaving 7.4% unemployed.

What occupational sectors did they go for?

In stark contrast to Economics, graduates in Geography go into a wide variety of occupations, some professional, others not. Retail, catering, waiting and bar staff is technically the biggest destination with 17.6% of employed graduates. A smaller proportion recurs approximately in four further occupational clusters. Commercial and public service manager jobs account for 13.1% and include traineeships with Abercrombie & Fitch, and policy officer with the Scottish Government. 13.3% went into other clerical and secretarial, 12.5% into other occupations, including Royal Marine in the Royal Navy. Business and financial professionals also accounted for 12.5%, and included jobs as auditor and trainee accountant with Lloyds TSB Bank plc and Ernst & Young respectively. Other professions included a number of jobs where the subject discipline was clearly relevant, such as trainee quantity surveyor and transport planner. Finally, education professionals took 4.64% and social professionals 32.9%, including community development worker for a local authority.

4.3 Law

Range

The range of Law degrees is not extensive, but does include degrees in Torts and Jurisprudence, and in topic areas such as Property, Medical or Criminal Law. There are also degrees on Law within a defined area: Scottish; English; EU; or Comparative Law.

Response rate and destination percentages

The response rate was 81.9% with a total of 10,155 graduates responding, making Law the biggest student body within Social Sciences. As with several other disciplines in this section, there were more female respondents than male respondents, with 6,385 female to 3,770 male respondents. 34.2% of these graduates were in UK employment, with a further 1.2% in overseas employment. 11.3% were combining work with studying. Added together, that makes 46.7% in employment. This relatively low employment rate is balanced by a very high study rate, particularly in the category 'UK further study' which accounts for 30.1% of all respondents. This is because many Law graduates undertake the vocational training needed for legal practice, typically the Legal Practice courses for Solicitors and the Bar Professional Training (known as Bar Vocational Training before the academic year 2010/11) for Barristers. 7.5% went on to study in the UK for a higher degree, which included LLM International Criminal Law and MA Human Resource Management. A further 0.5% were studying overseas, and 0.6% were studying for a teaching qualification, bringing the studying total to 38.7%. 3.5 % were unavailable for employment, study or training. 4.9% came into the 'other' category, leaving 6.2% unemployed.

What occupational sectors did they go for?

Given that over a third of these respondents proceeded to further training on graduation, there are relatively modest percentages in the employment sectors. It is interesting to see 13.4% working as legal professionals, doing jobs such as trainee solicitor and paralegal with various law firms. Although a small percentage, 2.5%, went into other professions, the relevance of the degree studied is evident in jobs such as immigration adviser with the Citizens Advice Bureau and welfare rights officer for local government. 7.1% went into business and finance professional jobs, including auditor with Deloitte and the National Audit Office. Commercial and public sector management accounted for 10.3% and other clerical and secretarial work accounted for a further 16.6%. 13.2% went into other occupations, and 21.5% into retail, catering, waiting and bar work.

4.4 Politics

Range

Politics courses include the study of politics in a given area such as the Commonwealth, the EU or simply International Politics. Courses also include the study of Political Systems and Theories in general or, in particular, for example, Fascism, Socialism or Anarchism. Courses can focus on the constitutional, including UK Government, Parliamentary Studies or Public Administration. War and Peace as a degree is also included here.

Response rate and destination percentages

A total of 3,910 graduates responded, a response rate of 79.5%. There were fewer female respondents than male respondents, with 1,645 female and 2,265 male respondents. Only Economics and Politics show this gender balance with males, in contrast with most of the disciplines in this section. 47.5% of these graduates were in UK employment, with a further 2.7% in overseas employment. 7.3% were combining work with studying. Added together, that makes 57.5% in employment. 15.3% went on to study in the UK for a higher degree, which included PhD South Asian Politics, MSc International Relations, MSc Marketing, and MA in Human Resources Management. 5.7% went on to further study in the UK including the graduate diploma in Law. 1.1% progressed to PGCE. 0.6% were studying overseas, bringing the studying total to 22.7%. 4.8 % were unavailable for employment, study or training. 4.6% came into the 'other' category, leaving 10.4% believed to be unemployed.

What occupational sectors did they go for?

Politics graduates went into a wide range of professional and managerial jobs. 15.8% went into commercial and public sector management, securing employment in Parliament, the Civil Service and the Foreign and Commonwealth Office. The biggest employment sector, at 18.7%, was retail, catering, waiting and bar work. 14.3% went into clerical and secretarial occupations for employers, including Oxfam and the Crown Prosecution Service. 11.2% were categorised as other occupations. 10.7% opted for business and financial professions, with employers here including Orange and Rothschild. Marketing, sales and advertising professions absorbed 9.8% of the employed graduates. Other professional occupations, at 6.3%, included varied work from overseas charity to recruitment consultancy.

4.5 Psychology

Range

Psychology degrees include subjects that reflect the range of applications in practice: Clinical, Educational, Health and Occupational Psychology, and the particular focus given to one aspect of the overarching discipline, such as Cognitive, Developmental, Experimental or Social. Neuropsychology and Psychometrics are also included here.

Response rate and destination percentages

Psychology is one of the largest student populations within Social Sciences (Law being the largest) and, with a total of 9,365 graduates responding, their response rate was 81.8%. There were 7,745 female and 1,620 male respondents; along with most of the degree disciplines in this section, women are in the majority. 55.2% were in UK employment, with a further 0.9% in overseas employment. 10.1% were combining work with studying. Added together, that makes 66.2% in employment. 10.3% went on to study in the UK for a higher degree, which included PhD Counselling Psychotherapy, Masters in Psychology specialisms such as Occupational, Health and Forensic Psychology, and MA Crime Law and Society. 3.2% progressed to PGCE, with 3.3% taking on other further study in the UK (including training for mental health nursing) and 0.1% studying overseas. The total percentage of graduates studying is 16.9%. 4.3% were unavailable for employment, study or training, 4.4% came into the 'other' category, leaving 8.3% reporting unemployed.

What occupational sectors did they go for?

The biggest single share of psychology graduates, some 24%, are found in other occupations. The British Psychological Society advises that only 15–20% of all those who graduate with a qualifying degree in Psychology will go onto to become professional psychologists. Many of those professional postgraduate training courses demand relevant work experience before admission, so it could be that graduates in these occupations are working to meet that requirement. Social and welfare professionals took 15.6%, including support worker in a range of settings, with Mencap, Mind and the NHS. A further 3% worked as health professionals, including psychological wellbeing practitioner for the NHS. 4% were in other professions, 4.1% in business and finance professions, 3.6% in marketing, sales, and advertising professions. 11.4% went into other clerical and 19% into retail, catering, waiting and bar staff. 6.8% secured work in commercial and public service management, with jobs including graduate traineeships in Specsavers and the Civil Service fast stream.

4.6 Sociology

Range

The range of courses included in Sociology is very wide indeed. It includes the sociology of science, of politics and of economics, the study of social theory, social hierarchy and of disability in society. Courses such as Men's Studies, Women's Studies or Gender Studies are here too, along with Applied Social Science.

Response rate and destination percentages

A total of 4,455 graduates responded, 78.8% of all graduates in this discipline. As in most of the Social Sciences, there were more female respondents than male respondents, with 3,390 female to 1,065 male respondents. 59.4% of these graduates were in UK employment, with a further 0.9% in overseas employment and 8.2% who were combining work with studying. Added together, that makes 68.5% in employment. 7.2% went on to study in the UK for a higher degree, which included PhD Social Anthropology, MA Media and Journalism, MA Criminology and Social Justice. 4% went on to further study in the UK and 3.1% progressed to PGCE with 0.1% studying overseas, bringing the studying total to 14.4%. 3.7% were unavailable for employment, study or training and 4% came into the 'other' category, leaving 9.5% reporting unemployed.

What occupational sectors did they go for?

Sociology graduates go into a wide variety of occupations, some professional, others not. Retail, catering, waiting and bar staff is technically the biggest destination with 23.7%. Other occupations account for 19.9%. Clerical and secretarial occupations took 14.3% and a similar proportion (14.5%) went into social and welfare professions, including support worker for youth offending. 2.6% went into other professions, including work in a housing association and a jobcentre. Business and finance professionals accounted for 4.9%. At 8% commercial and public service managers was a significant destination. 4% went into marketing and sales professionals, and 2.2% into education professions.

5 Arts, Creative Arts and Humanities

Six disciplines are included here, namely: Art and Design; English; History; Media Studies; Languages; and Performing Arts. From the respondents included in the sample, employment rates average 68% for Art and Design, Media Studies and Performing Arts. For English, History and Languages, the average is nearer 59%. The percentages going into study complement the picture: around 8% for Art and Design and Media Studies, about 16% for Performing Arts and averaging around 22% in the three other disciplines. Self-employment accounts for only 4.1% of all graduates from every single course – some 6,130 people. Of those budding entrepreneurs, 14.3% graduated from design subjects and a further 15% drawn evenly from Drama and Music disciplines.

You will notice that many graduates go into non-graduate jobs as their first destination; this year has seen an increase in retail, catering, waiting and bar work now accounting for anything from 16.5% of employed graduates from Languages to 29.9% in Media Studies. If it means anything, it means that these are just the first destinations, that graduates can use these jobs to develop skills and competence for leverage, that graduates might just enjoy this kind of work or that graduates might simply want to earn enough money to allow them to be creative – certainly the story of someone waiting on tables one day and being discovered the next has been a dream come true for more than one successful artist down the ages.

▶ brilliant example

'After my first year at a London dance conservatoire, I chose to transfer my studies
to university, in order to gain a more academic and theoretical knowledge of the
performing arts world. Whilst being able to continue building on technique and
performance quality through practical classes, the course also allowed me to
take an in-depth look at current practitioners and newly emerging dance makers,
whilst being pushed to take my particular research interest (dance in education)
further and further at each step of the course. Since graduating, I have worked as
a performer, choreographer and company manager on UK tours, danced on cruise
ships, and have recently taken over as principal of two part-time theatre schools
in London.'

Dan, BA (Hons) Performing Arts

5.1 Art and Design

Range

There is a range of disciplines under the Design umbrella, including:
Ceramics; Clothing; Fashion; Furniture; Graphic; and Industrial. This
in addition to the familiar domains of Painting, Printmaking, Illustration
and Sculpture. Moving away from the applied disciplines, more theoretical
courses are included, such as Fine Art Theory and Visual Communication.

Response rate and destination percentages

A total of 12,540 graduates responded, 80.7% of graduates in these
disciplines. There were 8,135 female and 4,405 male respondents. 61.7%
of these graduates were in UK employment, with a further 1.4% in overseas
employment. 5.8% were combining work with studying. Added together,
that makes 68.9% securing employment. 3.7% went on to study in the UK
for a higher degree, which included MA in Fine Art, Ceramics and Public
Relations. 2.4% went on to further study in the UK, 1.6% progressed to
PGCE. Very few were studying overseas, 0.1%, bringing the studying total
to just 7.8%. 4.2% were unavailable for employment, study or training,
6.3% came into the 'other' category, leaving 12.8% reporting unemployed.

What occupational sectors did they go for?

Of the graduates who went into employment, 32.2% went into arts, design, cultural and sports professionals. The destinations here clearly reflect the degrees studied: freelance model maker and interior designer. Retail, catering, waiting and bar staff accounted for a further 26%. Again, the relevance of degree discipline can be seen in jobs such as merchandiser for Liberty, and womenswear buyer for the Flannels Group. 13.5% are classified as 'other occupations' (including here trainee hair stylist) and 6.6% went into other clerical and secretarial work. Other professional and technical destinations (2.4%) included freelance prop and scene maker, cinema technician and art technician. Commercial and public sector management accounted for a further 6.3% and business and finance took just 1.6%.

5.2 English

Range

Degree courses in English cover English Language (including English as a second language), English Literature (including literature written in English as a second language) or a combination of both. Literature can be studied by period, by author, or by topic.

Response rate and destination percentages

A total of 8,545 graduates responded, 81.1% of all graduates in this category. As with every other discipline in this section, there were more female respondents than male respondents, with 6,345 female to 2,200 male respondents. With a female:male ratio of almost 3:1, English is the most gender imbalanced discipline in this broad sector. 49.9% of these graduates were in UK employment, with a further 2% in overseas employment. 8.3% were combining work with studying. Added together, that makes 60.2% in employment. 10.7% went on to study in the UK for a higher degree, which included PhD Linguistics, MAs in Acting and Film Studies, and Creative Writing. MSc courses included Business and Management. 5% went on to further study in the UK, and 5.8% progressed to PGCE. 0.3% were studying overseas, bringing the studying total to 21.8%. 4.3 % were unavailable for employment, study or training. 4.7% came into the 'other' category, leaving 9% reporting unemployed.

What occupational sectors did they go for?

The biggest single employment area is retail, catering, waiting and bar staff, at 23%. Next is other clerical and secretarial, with 15.1% of graduates employed. Other occupations accounted for a further 15.9% including here work as a royal marine. Turning to professional jobs, 9.3% went into education, including language assistant with the British Council. Commercial and public management took 7.9%, and included graduate traineeship with John Lewis. 7% went into marketing and sales professions, with jobs such as advertising sales coordinator with ITV and press officer with the BBC. A similar proportion, 6.6% went into art, design, culture and sports professions, including assistant editor for a publisher, and production assistant for the BBC. Business and accounting professions took 5.2% of those employed, and included KPMG and HSBC as employers. 4.3% became social and welfare professionals, and 2% went into other professions, including a policy internship in Brussels.

5.3 History

Range

History can be studied by period (e.g. Medieval, Ancient or Modern), by area (e.g. Welsh, Russian or New Zealand) or by topics such as Military History, Economic History, Social or Oral History.

Response rate and destination percentages

A total of 8,130 graduates responded, 83% of all graduates in this category. As with every other discipline in this section, there were more female respondents than male respondents, with 4,265 female and 3,860 male respondents. This makes history the most balanced discipline in terms of female:male participation rates. 47.1% of these graduates were in UK employment, with a further 2.2% in overseas employment. 7.8% were combining work with studying. Added together, that makes 57.1% in employment. 14.4% went on to study in the UK for a higher degree, which included MA Multimedia Broadcast Journalism and MA History. 6.1% went on to further study in the UK, including the graduate diploma in Law, and 3.5% progressed to PGCE. 0.4% were studying overseas, bringing the studying total to 24.4%. 4.7% were unavailable for employment, study or training. 4.5% came into the 'other' category, leaving 9.2% unemployed.

What occupational sectors did they go for?

History graduates went into a wide range of professional jobs. 10.3% went into commercial and public sector management, including management trainee with Enterprise Rent-a-car. 8.3% opted for business and financial professions, with employers here including HSBC, Deloitte and HM Revenue & Customs. Other professional occupations, at 3.9%, included being a proofreader and an auctioneer's assistant. Although a small proportion, 3.7%, secured employment as arts, design, culture and sports professionals, jobs here included editorial assistant with The History Press, and assistant in an art gallery. The biggest employment sector, at 23%, was retail, catering, waiting and bar work, followed by 17.9% in other occupations, which included personal trainer with Fitness First. 15% of employed graduates found work within clerical and secretarial occupations.

5.4 Media Studies

Range

The range of courses within Media Studies includes: Broadcasting; Film Production; Radio Production; and both TV and Screen Production. The focus of other courses is more towards what might be called the infrastructure behind the media production, including Electronic Media and Media Technology. A final segment within the subject area is degrees that take a critical overview through the study of: Film; Media; Culture; TV; Radio; and Communication. Typically, the degree title would be Media Studies.

Response rate and destination percentages

A total of 4,350 graduates responded, nearly 79.7% of all graduates in this category. There were more female respondents than male respondents: 2,310 female and 2,040 male respondents. 64% of these graduates were in UK employment, with a further 1.1% in overseas employment. 4.2% were combining work with studying. Added together, that makes 69.3% in employment. 4.4% went on to study in the UK for a higher degree, which included MA International Film Studies and MA Moving Image. 1.4% went on to further study in the UK, and 0.9% progressed to PGCE. 0.2% reported they were studying overseas, bringing the studying total to 6.9%. 4% were unavailable for employment, study or training. 5.3% came into the 'other' category, leaving 14.6% believed to be unemployed.

What occupational sectors did they go for?

At first glance, seeing 29.9% of graduates in this subject area going into jobs in retail, catering, waiting and bar staff, and a further 12.8% going into clerical and secretarial occupations, might confirm the idea that these degrees don't necessarily lead to graduate-level jobs. But remember that the data looks only at the first job on graduation, and remember too that many such graduates may be using their wages in this occupational sector to support themselves whilst working on breaking into their chosen field. If they do, they follow in the footsteps of many fellow graduates, as 14.7% secured professional jobs in arts, design, culture and sports. Within this, 3.9% went into broadcasting and 1.1% went into directing and producing. Jobs included theatre and creative directors, and studio manager and presenter for radio. 7.3% found a profession in marketing, sales and advertising, including web marketing officer in higher education, and media administrator for a charity. 8.1% went into commercial and public sector management roles and a relatively small proportion (3.6%) went into business and accounting professions.

5.5 Languages

Range

The range of languages includes the more familiar, e.g. French, the more exotic, e.g. African, and the more unexpected, e.g. both Cornish and Manx. As well as the study of foreign languages, the study of language itself is included, e.g. Phonetics or Phonology. It also includes the appreciation of what language can do, e.g. Latin Literature in Translation.

Response rate and destination percentages

A total of 6,835 graduates responded, some 82% of all graduates in this category. There were more than twice the number of female respondents than male respondents: 4,765 female to 2,070 male respondents. 43% of these graduates were in UK employment, with a further 9.1% in overseas employment. 7.6% were combining work with studying. Added together, that makes 59.7% employed. 10% went on to study in the UK for a higher degree, which included MA Applied Translation Studies, MSc Information Technology and LLM Human Rights. 6.4% went on to further study in the UK, and 5.4% progressed to PGCE. Just under 1% were studying overseas, bringing the studying total to just over 22.7%. 5.2% were unavailable for employment, study or training, 4.1% came into the 'other' category, leaving 8.3% believed to be unemployed. The overseas employment rate, at 9.1%, is the highest percentage of all degree disciplines. Could it be a case of 'have languages, will travel'?

What occupational sectors did they go for?

Looking more closely at those graduates who secured employment, the biggest proportion (16.5%) went into retail, catering, waiting and bar staff, with clerical and secretarial occupations close behind at 15.8%. There are three broad categories which each account for a similar proportion of these graduates. Management (both commercial and public sector) with 10.9%, business and finance also with 10.9%, and the catch-all of other occupations taking 13%. 6.6% were employed as education professionals, including teaching French in a secondary school. A further 6.2% went into arts, design, culture and sports professions, including freelance film producer and runner for a media production company.

5.6 Performing Arts

Range

It will come as no surprise that many of the degree disciplines included here cover performance: Acting; Dance; Musicianship or Performing; and Performing for the Theatre. There is another cluster of named degrees where the focus is on the creative input to a performance as a whole. These include: Directing for Theatre; Choreography; Stage Design; Theatre Design; Wardrobe Design and Theatrical Make-up. The final grouping focuses on the critical study of one or more of the performing arts within its context and history, namely History of Dance; History of Music; Musical Instrument History, and Theatre Studies.

Response rate and destination percentages

A total of 8,020 graduates responded, some 79.9% of all graduates in this category. There were more female respondents than male respondents: 4,870 female and 3,150 male respondents. 58.4% of these graduates were in UK employment, with a further 1.7% in overseas employment. 6.8% were combining work with studying. Added together, that makes 66.9% in employment. 7.5% went on to study in the UK for a higher degree, which included MA Acting, MA Music and MSc Air Transport Management. 4.3% went on to further study in the UK, including Community Theatre, and 4.1% progressed to PGCE. A mere 0.2% were studying overseas, bringing the studying total to 16.1%. 3% were unavailable for employment, study or training. 4.9% came into the 'other' category, leaving 9% believed to be unemployed.

What occupational sectors did they go for?

A satisfying 23% of these graduates secured work as professionals in the fields of art, design, culture and sports. Individual destinations included working as an actor with the RSC and as dancer and dance instructor. 22.3% went into retail and catering, a further 15% went into 'other occupations', and 8.4% into other clerical and secretarial occupations. 12.6% found work as education professionals, including education officer for a film festival. Other professions, at 1%, was a minority destination, but showed degree-relevant jobs such as acting with the National Youth Theatre and director's assistant in India.

6 Business and Administrative Studies

There are three subject areas included in this section, namely Accountancy, Business and Management, and Marketing. Compared with average employment rates for all graduates covering the full spectrum of degree courses, employment rates in these three disciplines are higher, with the average across the respondent samples coming in at around 73%. There is a clear relationship between the subject studied and the destination by occupational sector, e.g. 49% of the Accountancy graduates who reported finding employment went into business and finance professions, many as accountants. Beyond the predictable destinations there is a huge variety of occupations, though small percentages in each domain. The gender balance across the three areas is interesting: in Accountancy there are more males than females; in Marketing there are more females than males, and in Business and Management it is pretty evenly balanced, with males just tipping the balance by a margin of about 3%.

▶ brilliant example

'I thoroughly enjoyed my course; it combined both the theory and practical elements of the subject with lecturers that have both academic excellence and industry experience. A highlight for me was the work-based learning module – I found the exposure to the "real world" invaluable. Following graduation I used the confidence I gained to do the stereotypical post-university student activity: travelling. After seeing some of the sights the world had to offer, the job market was my destination. I secured a position with one of the world's biggest banks on their executive management graduate scheme, aimed at creating the next generation of company leaders.'

Phil, BA (Hons) Business Studies

6.1 Accountancy

Range

The range here is not extensive. Beyond Accountancy and Accounting, there are professional divisions including Cost and Management Accounting, and Public Accounting. Other specialisms include Book-keeping, Auditing of Accounts, Financial Reporting and Accounting Theory.

Response rate and destination percentages

A total of 3,200 graduates responded, 81.4% of all graduates in this category. There were fewer female respondents than male respondents: 1,350 female to 1,850 male respondents. 48.6% of these graduates were in UK employment, with a further 0.7% in overseas employment. 20.4% were combining work with studying. Added together, that makes 69.7% in employment. 4.7%

went on to study in the UK for a higher degree, which included MSc Finance, MSc Management and the specialist degree Master of Business Administration (MBA). 0.5% progressed to PGCE, and 4.9% went on to further study in the UK, with 0% studying overseas, bringing the studying total to 10.1%. 3.6% were unavailable for employment, study or training. 4% came into the 'other' category, leaving 12.5% believed to be unemployed.

What occupational sectors did they go for?

As could be expected, a very high proportion (44.2%) of these employed graduates secured employment as business and financial professionals and associate professionals. Job titles included trainee chartered accountant, assistant auditor and assurance technician. Chartered accountant was, however, the most common job, accounting for 21% of the graduates within this category. Employers included Ernst & Young and KPMG. Another 16.5% became numerical clerks and cashiers; while these were not graduate jobs, they would, nonetheless, provide valuable experience for graduates to move into a trainee professional role in due course. A further 7.6% went into commercial and public sector management, and 2.7% into the marketing, sales and advertising professions. 12.3% went into retail, catering, waiting and bar occupations, 7% into other clerical jobs and 6.3% fell into the catch-all category of 'other occupations'.

6.2 Business and Management

Range

This grouping spans Business Studies degrees, including European and International Business Studies. Management degrees include Management Studies and Management Techniques, followed by a spectrum of management specialisms and sectors: Change; Creative; Strategic; Domestic; Land; Project; Property; Retail; Hotel and Catering; and Recreational and Leisure. Valuation and Auctioneering caters for more of a niche market.

Response rate and destination percentages

A total of 14,155 graduates responded, 79.2% of all graduates in this category. There were fewer female respondents than male respondents, but a pretty even balance with 6,800 females and 7,355 males. 62.6% of these graduates were in UK employment, with a further 1.5% in overseas employment. 7.7% were combining work with studying. Added together, that makes 71.8% in employment. 5.5% went on to study in the UK for a higher degree, which included specialist Masters in Business Administration (MBA) and MSc Strategic Quality Management. 0.9% progressed to PGCE, and 2.2% went on to further study in the UK, with only 0.3% studying overseas, bringing the studying total to 8.9%. 4.3% were unavailable for employment, study or training. 5.2% came into the 'other' category, leaving 9.8% believed to be unemployed.

What occupational sectors did they go for?

A high proportion of Business and Management graduates found employment as either business and financial professionals and associate professionals (16.7%) or marketing, sales and advertising professionals (11.1%). Jobs included audit trainee, trainee accountant and bank analyst within business and finance, and account manager and junior market manager within marketing and advertising. Employers included: PricewaterhouseCoopers, Deutsche Bank, Rolls-Royce and Microsoft. A further 21.2% went into commercial and public sector management as trainees or a project manager for Red Bull. Clerical and secretarial occupations took a further 12%. 15.5% went into retail, waiting, catering and bar staff, 4.1% became numerical clerks and cashiers, with 9.6% going into other occupations, including work as an energy consultant.

6.3 Marketing

Range

The range of degrees included is not wide, comprising Marketing, International Marketing and Market Research, also: Advertising; Promotion and Advertising; Sponsorship; Corporate Image; Sales Management; and Distribution.

Response rate and destination percentages

A total of 2,415 graduates responded, 80% of all graduates in this category. There were more female respondents than male respondents, with 1,340 females to 1,075 males. 66.2% of these graduates were in UK employment, with a further 1.5% in overseas employment. 4.9% were combining work with studying. Added together, that makes 72.6% in employment. 4.8% went on to study in the UK for a higher degree, which included MSc in Business Management and in Technical Communications. 0.6% progressed to PGCE, and 1.8% went on to further study in the UK, with only 0.3% studying overseas, bringing the studying total to 7.5%. 4.4% were unavailable for employment, study or training. 5.2% came into the 'other' category, leaving 10.3% believed to be unemployed.

What occupational sectors did they go for?

The most common employment destination for marketing graduates was marketing, sales and advertising professionals, which accounted for 30.5% of the employed graduates, with employers ranging from an aerospace company to Kimberley-Clark. 16.3% went into commercial and public sector management, jobs here included policy adviser in HM Treasury and management trainee with Enterprise Rent-A-Car. Business and finance professions took another 6.8%, with jobs such trainee auditor for a borough council. Other clerical jobs accounted for 12.6%. 7.2% went into 'other occupations', including call centre operative, with 1.7% working as numerical clerks and cashiers. A significant proportion (17.6%) went into retail, waiting, catering and bar staff, including work as a supervisor with New Look.

7 Foundation degrees (all subjects studied at this level)

Defining characteristics of a Foundation degree

Foundation degrees were introduced in 2001. Although recognised as a qualification in its own right, a Foundation degree is designed to make it easy to lead onto an Honours degree. This means that a successful graduate from a Foundation degree may progress to level three (the final year for students studying full-time) and graduate in due course with Honours. Foundation degrees were intended to combine work-based learning with degree-level study and so include significant amounts of work-based learning. It is hardly surprising that the destinations data show roughly equal proportions of students (a) studying for their first degree, (b) combining work and study, and (c) securing employment in the UK. Destinations data are collected for all Foundation degree students but are not disaggregated by subject discipline.

▶ brilliant example

'As well as the huge variety of academic knowledge I gained on my Foundation degree, I also made a lot of personal developments which have really helped boost my confidence. I thoroughly enjoyed a work-based placement, learning a lot about the skills needed when working with animals, and experiencing the different issues that arise. My current role involves working with animals and continuing my learning of the technical side of animal management. I really enjoy my current role and look forward to continuing to work with animals and continuing my professional development.'

Jessica, FdSc, Animal Management

Response rate and destination percentages

There were 13,380 responses, 82.5% of all qualifiers in this category. There were more female respondents than male respondents, with 8,385 females to 4,995 males. 34.8% of these graduates were in UK employment, with only 0.3% in overseas employment. 23.4% were combining work with studying. Added together, that makes 58.5% in employment. 1.6% were unavailable for work or study and 4.4% come into the catch-all 'other' category. Only 2.7% were unemployed. Nearly 31% went on to study in the UK for a Bachelor's degree. BSc degree courses included: Quantity Surveying; Animal Science and Management; Civil Engineering; Ecology; and Geography. BA degree courses included: Multidisciplinary Healthcare; International Tourism Management; Art and Design; and Creative Media. A further 1.9% progressed to PGCE.

What occupational sectors did they go for?

Because the destination data are collected from the full range of Foundation degree courses studied, the destination occupations cover an extremely wide range of occupational sectors. Individual sectoral percentages are therefore so small as to be unhelpful in telling the story of the Foundation graduates.

CHAPTER 4

Graduate training schemes

This chapter covers one of the better-known options for graduates, and for many graduates it's the option they aspire to. In case you are not quite clear about what's involved, we will start with a definition, before looking at some examples. Finally, we will show you how to be a strong contender, if a graduate training scheme is your preferred option.

What is a graduate training scheme?

 **brilliant** definition

The term **graduate training scheme** is usually applied to graduate entry jobs, with training, in large organisations, both public and private sector – the kind you will meet at graduate recruitment fairs.

Sectoral growth and decline

Graduate training schemes can be found in a whole range of job areas, or sectors. Vacancies are currently on the increase in banking, financial services, insurance, business consulting, construction and accountancy. In other sectors, while there is an overall decline in vacancies, there are still opportunities to be found, for example in retail, investment banking, public sector, law, engineering and IT/telecommunications.

Note that the term graduate training scheme is sometimes used in professions like law, accountancy, teaching and psychology. In this chapter we are looking at more generalist schemes where the subject of your degree may be less important and the training more broadly based.

Direct entry

Many smaller organisations or SMEs (small to medium-sized enterprises) offer the same kind of opportunity for a graduate entrant, but may not label it a graduate training scheme. Remember that in Chapter 2 we defined an SME as an organisation with up to 250 employees. These organisations cover almost 60 per cent of the private sector employment in the UK and this includes graduate-level roles, with training.

On the other hand, be aware that many larger organisations also recruit people, who happen to be graduates, to what are called direct-entry jobs, where a degree is not a requirement. This might give you a route in, if your application for a graduate training scheme has been unsuccessful, and you could still work towards a position similar to someone who has come through the graduate training scheme route.

Three key features

The key defining features of a graduate training scheme are:

- You need a degree.
- You will follow a planned programme which will enable you to sample different work areas and identify your particular strengths and interests.
- You will be employed and therefore paid a salary.

... and three myths

- Graduate training schemes usually lead to a job – but not automatically. You may have to apply for internal vacancies, or wait until a suitable role comes up. In some cases, especially in the public sector, graduate training schemes are offered on a fixed-term contract and offer no guarantee of a job.

- You have to go straight into a graduate training scheme as soon as you leave university. Not so – many graduates apply in the year following graduation – or even later than that. Employers are fine with this, as long as you can show some benefit to yourself, and potentially to the employer, deriving from the time since you graduated. Typically, around half of all graduate trainees recruited across the UK will not be straight from university.

- You have to have a first class or upper second class Honours degree. Not so – although some companies have such a requirement, many do not.

Some typical graduate training schemes

These examples come from recently advertised graduate training schemes, and help to illustrate the features they have in common, and where the differences might be. You will see that even this small sample covers a range of occupational areas and includes an SME.

 **examples**

A UK clothing company

- Offers an 18-month scheme involving Design, Development, Marketing and Merchandising.

- Applicants need a degree in Footwear, Fashion, Business or Marketing; work experience in fashion retailing or customer service; and competency in MS Office.

- An interesting additional requirement is that they must have delivered profit in a venture, whether commercial, voluntary or university-based.

A large, national public sector organisation

- A two-year scheme in which graduates choose one of four areas: human resources, finance, infomatics or general management, in each case leading to a professional qualification.

- Before specialising they have a grounding in all four areas. There are several work placements of up to nine months each.

- Applicants need a 2:2 or better in any subject. The organisation states that successful trainees can expect to fast-track their career development.

A large, multinational packaging company

- Recruits finance, business, research and engineering specialists.

- Every graduate trainee takes part in a standard induction programme. This is followed by individually tailored training plans, all of which will include key business and interpersonal skills.

- Finance and engineering trainees follow approved professional training, while business trainees have a series of secondments to different management functions.

- Graduates of all disciplines can apply; the company looks for good interpersonal skills and a genuine interest in a career in the manufacturing industry.

A small to medium-sized enterprise (SME)

- This software and consulting company offers the benefits of a graduate training scheme in a smaller organisation (fewer than 250 employees).

- You would need a 2:1 or better and As and Bs at A level (or the equivalent), good interpersonal skills, an interest in IT and finance and evidence of outstanding academic achievement.

- A five-week induction programme begins a two-year curriculum with in-house and external training to provide a mix of technical, functional and soft skills. There is financial support to gain further qualifications, ranging from foreign languages to financial diplomas and technical accreditations.

Is a graduate training scheme right for you?

Meeting the selection criteria

The harsh reality is that, in order to deal with large numbers of applications, recruiters to graduate training schemes set the bar high in terms of degree classification and sometimes even UCAS points. Sometimes the initial selection is done using computer software. This is highly likely to be the case if you apply online. If you don't meet an essential requirement (for example, you have a 2:2, they want a 2:1) you will be selected out. They may even use UCAS points as a selection tool. And all this will happen well before anyone reads your well-crafted personal statement. So you need to consider if, and how, you can achieve what is being asked for. If you can't, then look for other routes.

brilliant example

A large, multinational business consultancy has an alternative graduate training scheme for people who have fallen short of the academic standards normally required but can demonstrate achievement outside their studies.

In large organisations you need to be prepared for, and willing to commit to, the full range of selection methods. The entire selection process could last a full day or more and may even require an overnight stay. Have a look at Chapter 9 'Dates and deadlines: your timeline for action' for managing all this alongside your study, and Chapter 11 'Succeeding in selection', for more about what might be involved.

A chance to find your strengths and interests

You may know that you would like to work in a large organisation of a particular kind – public sector, logistics, retail, finance – but not yet be clear about a specific direction. Many graduate training schemes offer a programme of rotation through various functions and, while you will be expected to make a contribution in each area you work in, you do have the chance to experience different roles first hand.

Are you flexible?

Large, multi-site organisations will expect you to be prepared to work at different locations. Even if the head office is in your home town, it doesn't mean that you will work there. Make sure you are aware of any requirements to move or work away, and that they fit with your own circumstances.

Can you commit?

A graduate training scheme is long term – think two years minimum, and that's just for the training programme. So, if you plan to work for six months and then travel, it's not for you at this stage. A recruiting organisation wants a return for the cash investment it's making in selection and training – and you will be giving a lot of yourself to get the most from the experience. So be sure that the time is right for you.

How to be a strong contender for a graduate training scheme

Much of what we say elsewhere in this book, about researching the labour market, job opportunities, applications and interviews, applies to graduate training schemes as well as to other options you may be considering, so we will assume that you will dip in to the relevant chapters as you need to. What we will do here is look at the particular demands of graduate training schemes on you, the applicant.

Know the business in context

For every organisation you apply to, you need to know how they generate their revenue, who their competitors are, how they adapt to changes in the market, their strengths, what they are developing, and so on. This knowledge will help you with your application and certainly with your interview. Visit careers fairs, look at websites, talk to anyone who might know anything about the organisations or the sectors they belong to.

Know about recruitment timescales and where to find vacancies

Some graduate training schemes have an annual or twice yearly intake, others a rolling programme. For the first group, being ready to apply at the right time is critical. Sign up for careers fairs, pick up your free copies of graduate directories (a key source for graduate training schemes) from your careers service, use graduate recruitment websites.

It doesn't matter what the business is, there are some fundamental principles: cash flow is king; you've got to make sure there's a bottom line for the profit, and you've got to look at risk. Graduates need to ask where they fit into the critical path within the business process.

Julian Radley, Finance Director, Evotel Holdings

Know about selection methods

We said earlier that graduate training schemes often use the full range of selection methods, in particular assessment centres, so make sure you know what these are, what to expect and how to prepare for them. Read Chapter 11 'Succeeding in selection', for lots more information about this.

Be creative

If you don't meet the academic requirements, is there another way you can gain access? You could look for companies like the brilliant example earlier in this chapter, or you could try a direct approach with a good letter or personal contact at a careers fair. Alternatively you could go for direct entry and aim to progress once you are in the organisation.

Manage your applications

You will almost certainly be applying to more than one graduate training scheme, so keep your applications in order – create a schedule of closing dates and interview dates, make an electronic or paper folder to keep copies of applications, CVs and interview information. Read Chapter 9 'Dates and deadlines' for more about managing your time to hit closing dates and keep your academic work going at the same time.

Seek and make use of feedback

An unsuccessful application can help you to get the next one better. We talk about this in Chapter 10. If you get as far as an interview you should be able to ask the employer for feedback – but do listen to what is said. The employer is telling you how you presented at interview, so try not to defend or justify, because it really doesn't matter – what matters is what the employer saw and heard.

 **brilliant** timesaver

Keep track by making a paper or electronic folder for copies of application forms, CVs and interview information.

brilliant dos and don'ts

Do

✔ find out about the business and its competitors;

✔ learn about selection methods;

✔ get and use feedback;

✔ look for different routes to where you want to be.

Don't

✘ leave it till the last minute to look for vacancies;

✘ lose track of your applications.

What are the benefits?

We think there are three key benefits of graduate training schemes, and we are not alone. Have a look at the three real-life graduate stories that follow.

In our first example, Paul highlights the benefits of learning to work in a big organisation.

brilliant example

'My role as a trainee manager on the graduate training scheme of an international car rental company provides me with valuable training on running a business, working as a manager and working your way up a big organisation. The experience has given me such a big insight into the workings of a big company.'

Paul, BSc (Hons) Sport and Exercise Science

In our next example you can see that a good graduate training scheme will support you in further learning, sometimes leading to specialist qualifications.

 **example**

'I secured a position with one of the world's biggest banks on their executive management graduate scheme. At university we were introduced to the concept of lifelong learning and with the bank I have the chance to further my studies with qualifications in financial services.'

Phil, BA (Hons) Business Studies

Our final example illustrates the longer-term benefits. Victoria's experience helped her to develop strengths and preferences that enabled her to work out the next stage of her career plan. She is now in her third job after graduating.

 **example**

'I joined the graduate programme of a consulting company. In two years I learned masses and I still use the tools and skills I gained with them. I use their methods as a mark of what good looks like in my present company. The IT projects I worked on were for a range of blue chip retail companies. However, after two years I wanted to try a move away from IT so I moved to another consultancy for more analysis and strategic projects . . . after another two years I realised that I wanted to work in retail, and within the industry rather than through consultancy. Because of my experience I found the job market very responsive, and I got my present job as a business systems analyst with a multinational retail organisation. I get to travel and work with different cultures, teaching and shaping how countries do business.'

Victoria, MA Geography

 **recap**

Graduate training schemes are great for developing your skills and experience. They help you to refine your career plans, and often include the chance for you to gain a specialist qualification.

What to do next

- Remind yourself of the key features of a graduate training scheme. Could you see yourself as a graduate trainee?

- Think about a job area you might like to work in – marketing, finance, research and development, HR – and see if you can find a suitable graduate training scheme being advertised. Visit websites; useful ones include **www.milkround.com** and **www.prospects.ac.uk**.

- Get hold of a copy of a directory of graduate training schemes from your careers service. Have a browse and look for similarities and differences among different schemes.

- Sign up for the next graduate careers fair in your area. Find out more from your university website or from **www.prospects.ac.uk**.

CHAPTER 5

The global graduate: travel and employability

If you are to genuinely understand about the things that really matter, about culture, then language is a barrier unless you have some understanding.

Carl Gilleard, Chief Executive, Association of Graduate Recruiters

You will see from the title of this chapter that we are looking at travel here from an employer's perspective. Employers are increasingly explicit about valuing a jobseeker who has had overseas experience, either through study or professional work. Our brilliant quote here relates to the employer's view of the global graduate being someone who has cultural awareness, and maybe language proficiency, over and above what other graduates offer. The focus here is how your experience abroad works for you in terms of enhancing your employability. This applies even if enhancing your employability was the last thing on your mind when you set off on your travels. This chapter works through why you might want an overseas experience, and how that overseas experience can enhance your employability. We also give an overview of what opportunities there are abroad, and how you would go about getting what is out there. Finally, we go through the practical steps you can take before, during and after your travels.

It doesn't matter why you want to travel

What we are looking at here is travelling and working or studying. These are not mutually exclusive: you can do them at the same time, but you are likely to be driven more by one or the other. So either you want to travel, and working or studying is just a way of satisfying your wanderlust, or you want to work, and are happy to take up employment outside your normal country of residence. You may even find that you enjoy the work as much as you enjoy the location: a brilliant combination.

The reasons people give for travelling are many and varied. Sometimes they can be negative:

> I was unhappy with my situation here; I needed to get away; I wanted to start afresh somewhere.

Sometimes they can be positive:

> I want to experience a different culture; I want to learn a new language; I want to live in the city/country/by the sea/in the mountains.

Sometimes, they can be explicitly about enhancing your professional repertoire:

> If I want to specialise in international economics, it makes sense to get first-hand experience of another economy.

It may just be that you feel like it, or the opportunity came your way.

 **brilliant tip**

It really doesn't matter why you want to travel. There doesn't have to be a rational reason: it is OK to travel just because you feel like it.

It doesn't really matter why you want to travel, and once you are caught up in the practicalities of booking flights, thinking about accommodation and working out what the work options are, thinking about what you do once you come back from your travels might be the very last thing on your mind. However, once you are back on the labour market and find yourself competing with other job seekers who haven't clocked up the air miles, it may matter a lot.

 **tip**

No matter what made you work, study or travel abroad, you are likely to develop (as a result) transferable skills that employers value.

Looking at travel from the employer's perspective

Employers value the transferable skills you will develop abroad

Once you're putting your travels behind you and are applying for work or postgraduate study, it is not about where you went and what you saw: it is how you expanded your professional repertoire and how you can apply what you learned on your travels to your new work situation. It is highly likely that you develop valuable transferable skills through your overseas experience. Chapter 2 takes a detailed look at what transferable skills are, but the most likely skills you will develop as a direct result of your overseas experience are:

- **Self-management**: you will have learnt more about yourself, about how you handle stress and being out of the familiar, or being out of your comfort zone. You may also have had time to think through what is important to you in your life and therefore in your career.

- **Problem solving**: no doubt your overseas experience threw up challenges and problems that you had to solve. Even relatively simple challenges inherent in travel (planning journeys, making connections, getting to the right place at the right time) will make you think through what you are doing and how you are doing it. You may well have found yourself dealing with the unfamiliar and perhaps the unexpected; this in turn demands you find a way through problems.

- **Resilience**: this is the capacity to keep going even when the going gets tough. Living, working, studying and travelling overseas can all be delightful, but can also be challenging. Resilience is how you handle yourself when things seem to be relentlessly challenging. This calls for hope, optimism and being prepared to reframe things mentally.

- **Foreign languages**: frankly, if you come back from an overseas experience with absolutely zero development in your language ability, that's disappointing. Even if you have mastered nothing but very basic language (greetings, thanks, requests) you will have had the valuable experience of realising how limited you are without language. And for many, the overseas experience allows you to develop fluency and understanding of the language in question and, through that, to develop an appreciation of culture and customs.

Employers value subject-specific skills

Our next brilliant example is interesting because Katie already has a job, as a lecturer in animal management at a college of further education. She is travelling in order to enrich her subject knowledge.

 **example**

'During the summer I plan to travel to Africa to work on an animal conservation project. I am so excited! I look forward to visiting this extraordinary country and working with fellow conservation lovers, caring for wild animals and helping to maintain their environment. I can put my passion into practice and continue to learn in breathtaking surroundings with some of the most magnificent animals.'

Katie, BSc (Hons) Animal Behaviour and Welfare

Employment that demands working abroad

For some people, their career goal is to take up a role that will, by definition, involve working abroad. Examples include teaching English abroad, working for the European Union, or simply working in the profession for which they have been trained, but in another country. A growing number of people are choosing to work in international development, an interest that may start though volunteering and develop into a paid role. Our next brilliant example, Rachel, spent half of the second year of her degree as an English language assistant in Réunion and Madagascar. She returned to Madagascar as a volunteer soon after graduation, working on building and reforestation projects. After a spell back home to earn some money, she returned to Madagascar, and she continues her story.

brilliant example

'I led a community health team in a remote region. I did a lot of translating as I was the only French speaker . . . I followed an ecology course as an independent student, being taught by non-government organisation (NGO) professionals . . . on my return to the UK I applied to an international relief and rehabilitation organisation. After a week-long assessment process, I was offered my present post in the Democratic Republic of Congo. I work in French every day, working in medical logistics.'

Rachel, BA (Hons) French and International Development Studies

What opportunities are there abroad?

Erasmus: short-term study abroad as part of your degree

Erasmus is arguably the best-known university exchange programme: over 1 million students have participated in the last 20 years. Under the Erasmus scheme, students spend at least one term studying in a different university in another country. The scheme has operated in at least 28 countries across the European Union (EU) and Switzerland and has recently expanded beyond the EU to other countries all over the world under the Erasmus Mundus scheme.

Erasmus eligibility requirements

In order to participate, you must be: enrolled as a student (undergraduate, postgraduate or doctoral); eligible to participate (which means, broadly speaking, that you should have the right to study in the EU); and your home university (here in the UK) must have a bilateral agreement with the host university (overseas). Your course tutor would know if a bilateral agreement with another university is already in place for the course you are on. Your own department might also have some information, but do look both at departmental and university level for the fullest possible information. Even if nothing is in place for your course, your university might already have a bilateral agreement with another university for other courses, and it could be possible for your subject simply to be added to that bilateral agreement.

So, if you are interested, the best place to start is the international office or possibly the Erasmus office in your own university. They should be able to advise you on what you can study where, and whether you can apply for a grant. Of course, what you make of those opportunities, and how you transfer your learning to your brilliant jobsearch, is very much up to you. Most of what we discuss in this chapter would apply to people taking part in an Erasmus programme: studying abroad gives you a unique opportunity to learn another language, to learn about another culture and to broaden your outlook.

Work experience as part of your degree

Some courses, especially language degrees, include a chance to spend a year working abroad in a role that will complement the academic content of the course, for example as an English language assistant in a school or college. Others may offer a shorter period of time – the kind of experience Joanne talks about.

brilliant example

'One of the modules I undertook on my course was called experiential learning. I had the opportunity to work in Romania, delivering drama workshops in communities and schools there. This opened my eyes to all sorts of valuable experiences and taught me so much about education in another country.'

Joanne, BA (Hons) Drama and Theatre Studies

Vacation work while you are a student

Most students need to work in the summer vacation, so why not think about working abroad? There are useful reference books on the subject which you will find in your university careers service or library, and some employers come onto campus to recruit.

▶ brilliant example

'The university careers team were instrumental in helping me secure a vacation job coaching football in the USA for the summer of my first year, something which undoubtedly benefited me and increased my employability.'

Phil, BA (Hons) Business Studies

How to get what's out there

Check if you are allowed to work

You can either secure employment and then travel to your new job – or travel to your destination first, then sort out employment. In some cases, you'll have to get the job first because that's what the law requires. You will find there are restrictions to employment depending on the country of employment and the nationality of the employee, so your normal country of residence is important.

There are, however, many opportunities: European Union (EU) nationals are free to live and work anywhere in the EU; some labour markets allow fixed-term work visas for temporary work, or specialised work that can't readily be filled by a local employee; and some international employers can secure work permits for employees who need them.

brilliant tip

European Union nationals are free to live and work anywhere in the European Union. In addition, temporary work visas are sometimes available for specified workers, either with key skills or in hard-to-fill sectors.

Before taking on employment you will need to check (a) if there are any restrictions and (b) if these restrictions apply to you. This information is readily available by country – though of course it may not be available in English. The best source of reliable information is the Embassy or High Commission of the country you are interested in. There are also compendium books which pull together a number of destination countries. Your university careers service should have these for reference.

Check out job opportunities

Chapter 1 takes you through the process of finding out what jobs are on offer in great detail, and everything in that chapter applies here. Broadly speaking, you need to look at what's on offer in terms of paid work, and you need to let employers know that you are available for work. You can use printed media (newspapers, bulletins and directories) and online media (websites, social networking, RSS feeds). Online is particularly useful for overseas work.

 **tip**

Make full use of online resources when looking for work abroad. Use websites, including national newspapers which publish job adverts online. Use social networks to find out about working abroad.

You can also look for work on location. If, for example, you are an EU citizen, you can travel anywhere within the EU and then look for a job. You can try the usual labour market channels: local newspapers; employment agencies; speculative applications (i.e. going into an organisation and asking them if they have any vacancies); or word of mouth. It is worth expanding your jobsearch to include some sectors and occupations you wouldn't normally think of; this is particularly useful if the experience of living and working abroad is more important than developing a particular set of job-related competencies.

The problem with looking for a job once you're abroad is that you'll need to stay somewhere, and to fund yourself during your period of jobsearch. This takes money – almost always more than you expect; and it probably takes a fairly good idea of the local job market, and maybe even a bit of luck once you get there to secure the kind of job you want, as shown in our brilliant example.

 **example**

'I started off looking for a job on the Mediterranean coast, because I'd got the chance of accommodation there. So basically I got a load of CVs and went round to pretty much every restaurant; because that was where I had had most experience, through my Saturday job and work experience at school. It was horrible, really scary, because I didn't really know what I was saying (in French). One place phoned back, invited me for an interview, and gave me a job as a runner.'

Hannah, (Undergraduate) Economics and Politics with International Studies

Check out whether casual work is worth the risks

Beware that you might be offered casual work that is not legitimate. This can be very tempting: often the pay is cash in hand and, at first sight, it does look so much easier to get started working straight away, rather than wade through the hassle of bureaucracy. But working illegally can end up being way more hassle. With no legitimacy and therefore no employment rights or protection, you would be on your own if you had to deal with some of the potential problems of unregulated employment: under payment; accidents at work; bullying; or discrimination.

brilliant tip

Take the bureaucracy of labour laws (work permits) seriously: protect yourself from the potential problems of unregulated work.

What you need to know before you go

The Foreign & Commonwealth Office (FCO) spearheads the 'Know Before You Go' Campaign, which aims to help British nationals to stay safe (and in good health) when abroad. It covers a number of key areas – some of which could save your life:

- get adequate travel insurance;
- check the FCO's country travel advice: this is updated very frequently, to take account of emergency situations, e.g. natural disaster or political unrest;
- research your destination – know the local laws and customs;
- visit your GP as soon you know that you are travelling;
- check your passport is in good condition and valid and you have all necessary visas;
- make copies of important travel documents and/or store them online using a secure data storage site;
- tell someone where you are going and leave emergency contact details with them;
- take enough money and have access to emergency funds.

 **tip**

Use the Foreign & Commonwealth Office (FCO) website (**www.fco.gov.uk**) for good information and advice about your destination.

Once you're away from home

Enjoying the overseas experience

You might find that the whole experience of working and living away from home is enjoyable from day one: that's brilliant! However, you also might have to put a bit of work into making the experience enjoyable.

Having some language is going to help – and acquiring language once you are there will help even more. Being ready to try new things, eat new food, do things in a new way is also going to help you adjust quickly and fit in. You might also need to make more of an effort to make new friends than you would do at home, just carrying on with your normal social circle. People may well make the first approach to include you in what they are doing, but you'll need to show that you are interested in what's going on and are prepared to fit in. So, try to accept any invitations – even if they turn out to be less than brilliant, you will at least have clocked up one more experience.

 **tip**

Be prepared to put a bit of effort into fitting in: try to pick up some language even if you feel self-conscious. Rather than dismissing an invitation or a suggestion, try to give new things a go.

Surviving the overseas experience

Thanks to social networking sites, you can learn a huge amount, both positive and negative, from other people's experiences. Use them to post questions in advance of your trip, and once you get to your new place. Once there, you can readily tap into the online community, which itself can be a mixture of local people and a more international crew. Your new work mates may also have good advice, which can cover really basic stuff (where to buy food at local supermarkets or markets) to blending in as a local (what are the unwritten rules about dress codes or local etiquette).

Bureaucracy and accessing key documents wherever you are

Once you are away from home, there are a number of really vital documents which, if lost, you would have to replace. Some of these are official: National Insurance documents; passport; visas. Others personal but equally important: insurance policies; tickets; bank details. You can easily create a document that records all the detailed information you would need if the worst were to happen. It will help enormously if you have someone back home who can access the things you need that you have forgotten to bring: your contact lens prescription; your birth certificate; your European Computer Driving Licence certificate. You could also scan these, and other important documents, and save them on an Internet-accessible website account that you can then access from an Internet connection anywhere in the world. Here's Hannah again.

 **example**

'The bureaucracy (for working abroad) was tedious, but not impossible. Both my employers did what they could to help. If I needed something I didn't have with me, I phoned home and got it faxed out, or went to an Internet café and accessed stuff that way.'

Hannah, (Undergraduate) Economics and Politics with International Studies

Keeping going when the going gets tough

Even if you have really been looking forward to going abroad, you will have difficult times, when you might feel lonely or homesick. You might feel you have made a big mistake and just want to go home. You might feel you are doing everything you possibly can to get work, make friends, join in with people and it's just not getting you where you want to be as fast as you want to get there. This is perfectly normal, and part of any successful transition from one phase of your life to another.

Positive steps to take

Try to keep a sense of perspective: is the setback you're experiencing going to be such a big deal in five days' or in five months' or even in five years' time? When you feel you've had a really rubbish day, just take five minutes on your own and identify three positive things that have happened. These can be quite small steps, for example:

> I got off the bus at the right bus stop/I understood my colleague when he asked me to do something.

Positive things can also be outside work, for example:

> I smelt the gardenia in blossom/I felt so warm in the heat of the day.

It can help to write these down in a notebook, so that you build up a store of positive experience, which can help to give a sense of perspective when you're feeling down. Try to keep going: put a bad day behind you and, rather than starting the next day convinced things are going to keep going wrong, try to be positive and open about this day going a little bit better.

 **tip**

Try to put negative experiences and feelings to one side and focus on the positive. Take five minutes, each and every day, to identify three positive experiences, no matter how small they may seem.

Returning

Securing something to come back to: study or work

Update your CV in the light of your experience abroad

Try to capture, on your CV and in your job applications, the ways in which you have expanded your skills and competence. If you have been working, your new skills may well be specific to the work you did, for example:

> I learned to speak fluent Spanish; I can cash up a till; I can operate tools and/or machinery and/or programmes.

Have a look at the kind of employability skills all employers want, but also look at anything an employer specifies in a job advert or person specification.

> **brilliant tip**
>
> Rethink your CV in the light of your travelling experience. Think it through from an employer's perspective so you are ready to explain how your travels have added value to you as a prospective employee.

Include soft skills: look at it from the employer's perspective

You may also have developed the so-called soft skills, which are just as sought after by employers. These include:

- communication;
- problem solving;
- self-management; and
- resilience.

It is highly likely that you will have found yourself in situations abroad where you had to be flexible, and perhaps also where you had to keep going when things weren't plain sailing. Teamwork skills, such as persuading/negotiating and respecting others, are undoubtedly skills you had to develop for a good experience abroad. Try to sell your experiences in terms that an employer will buy.

Foreign language ability

Many employers are not satisfied with foreign language fluency in graduates. However, before you claim you can negotiate high-level deals in another language, appraise your language levels. If your newly polished language is restricted to ordering food and drink, you might think about picking up some more commercial language applications as part of your jobsearch.

Get your return destination sorted before you go abroad

Securing a job or place on a postgraduate programme to pick up on your return is exactly the same procedure you followed to get your job abroad – but in reverse. You might be able to get this all sorted before you even go off on your travels, which means you don't have to think about it at all once you're away from home. Or you might decide to apply from abroad before you return. This is certainly worth exploring for postgraduate programmes, as an interview is not always necessary.

How to be interviewed at a distance

Even if you are expected to have an interview, you could explore the possibility of doing the interview at a distance – by Skype, for example. This would mean you would miss out on the chance to visit the campus and to meet other people applying for your programme, so it does have its drawbacks. However, the distance interview does have the major advantage of sparing you the expense of travelling a long way. If you do manage to organise a cyber-interview, treat it exactly as you would a face-to-face meeting: prepare for it thoroughly, and present yourself well. Dress formally, look professional. You can always head for the beach once the Internet interview is over.

 **tip**

If you need to be interviewed while you are abroad, ask if an online interview is possible, e.g. using Skype. Remember this is still a formal interview, so dress professionally and present yourself well.

Aftermath

 **tip**

Don't be too shocked if home seems unfamiliar when you first return: you will adjust to the way of life here, just as you did abroad!

Reverse culture shock

Coming home after a spell abroad might seem like the easiest thing in the world, but you need to be aware of reverse culture shock. Quite simply, what has always seemed familiar becomes unfamiliar when you go back to it, having experienced something quite different. You might even feel a bit homesick for your life abroad. This can come as something of a shock and, although it's not something people talk about very much, it is quite common. You can draw on the same techniques as you did when you were away: look for the positive in your experiences, however small, that may at first appear. You will adjust and, in time, things will fall into place again. Just hold on to everything that was good about your experience. Here's a final word from Hannah.

brilliant example

'The best thing about working abroad is when you realise that this is your life. You really do have friends here that you care about. You can go out with them and you can really talk to them in French. And it's as real a relationship as if it was in English. It's just very satisfying, and it's what I wanted. Would I recommend working abroad? Yes, definitely, one hundred per cent.'

Hannah, (Undergraduate) Economics and Politics with International Studies

brilliant recap

- Working abroad can be both enjoyable and useful.

- Just a few simple steps will help you to be safe and healthy.

- There are opportunities before, during and after your degree course.

- Make sure that you show clearly how your experiences add value to you as a prospective employee, using the language of employability and skills.

What to do next

Have a look at the Erasmus programme (**www.eu-student.eu**) to get an idea of what it does. You could also find out what your university offers under the Erasmus scheme, by talking to your course tutor, or the international or Erasmus office in your university. Use social networks or ask friends who have worked abroad what they made of the experience. Ask employers (at job fairs or alumni events) whether they value overseas experience. Simply think about travelling to enhance your employability, and keep it in mind as a possible option.

CHAPTER 6

Postgraduate study: choosing a course and making a good application

W e've already identified postgraduate study as one of the options you can choose from on completing your first degree. This chapter considers this option in more detail and, even if you have already made the decision to progress onto postgraduate training, you'll still find some of the later sections within this chapter useful.

Firstly, we consider the range of postgraduate courses on offer: academic and professional; full-time and part-time; distance, online and blended study modes; in the UK or overseas. Then we work through your decision-making process: the advantages and disadvantages of studying beyond an undergraduate degree; thinking through timing – whether to undertake postgraduate study immediately after your undergraduate degree or a few years into your career; finding out what you need to know before you commit to a particular programme; how to fund yourself as a postgraduate student, and how to make a good application. The final section talks you through presenting your postgraduate qualification in a positive light to an employer when making a job application.

Postgraduate courses – what's the range on offer?

The undergraduate degree as the basis for postgraduate study

It is safe to assume that you now know that an undergraduate degree is usually the first level of study you can undertake at a university. On successful completion you are awarded a Bachelor's degree, most commonly Bachelor of Arts (BA), Bachelor of Science (BSc) or a protected, specialist title such as Bachelor of Laws (LLB) or Bachelor of Medicine (MB). There are some slight distinctions within undergraduate degrees (foundation, ordinary and honours) but they are all undergraduate or first degrees. Once you have successfully completed your undergraduate degree, you can progress onto a higher level. It is worth noting that some postgraduate courses will consider an applicant without a first degree. This is more common on vocational courses where relevant work experience counts a lot.

Higher-level degrees: Masters and Doctoral

Masters degrees

There are two higher degree levels, namely: Masters and Doctoral. Masters degrees are awarded after a programme of teaching or research, or a mixture of the two. Typically, a Masters degree takes at least one year of full-time study. This can often be a full calendar year, lasting 12 months, as opposed to a full academic year. Students may work through the summer period (June/July/August) to produce an extended piece of independent work. The nature of their finished product will vary according to discipline, but it could be a research dissertation, an industrial or design project, or a performance piece.

Academic and professional Masters

A Masters degree can be designed as an academic programme, which allows you to study your chosen subject in more detail and depth, e.g. French Studies or Violence and Conflict. It might also be designed to satisfy a professional body's requirements for a qualifying examination, e.g. Architecture. Or it could be a programme of advanced study, with the possibility of researching an area of professional practice for qualified professionals who want a higher degree, e.g. Renewable Energy and the Built Environment. Some subjects are offered as a four-year programme, where students spend the first three years getting their first degree, and on successful completion progress onto their Masters, e.g. Civil Engineering courses leading to a Master of Engineering (MEng).

 **tip**

If you are thinking of a professional career, check what qualifications you need with the relevant professional body. They usually list courses they have approved.

Masters titles

Research-based programmes lead to the award of MPhil. Taught programmes most commonly lead to the award of Master of Arts (MA) or Master of Science (MSc), with specialist designated awards for professional qualifications such as Master of Engineering (MEng).

Postgraduate Certificate and Postgraduate Diploma

Studying at Masters level can also lead to the award of a Postgraduate Diploma or a Postgraduate Certificate. A diploma course typically takes one academic year studying full-time and a Postgraduate Certificate typically takes one term studying full-time, which equates to one academic year if you study part-time. Postgraduate Diplomas and Certificates are frequently awarded for programmes of study that are approved by a professional body. This means that, on completion of that programme, students will have reached a level of competence, making them equipped for professional practice. For example, the Postgraduate Diploma in Information Management at the University of Strathclyde is recognised by the Chartered Institute of Library and Information Professionals.

brilliant definition

Higher degrees can be academic or vocational/professional. Study at Masters level can lead to the award of Masters degree, Postgraduate Diploma or Postgraduate Certificate.

Doctoral degrees: research and taught (professional) doctorates

Research doctorate

Doctoral studies are research-based, and a doctorate is awarded, broadly speaking, for the creation of knowledge. The degree awarded would typically be a DPhil or a PhD, and would normally take three years of full-time study. It can of course be studied part-time.

Taught or professional doctorate

Where a doctoral programme includes a research component, but has a substantial taught element, this would lead to an award that specifies the discipline in the title, e.g. Doctor of Education (Ed D). These kinds of programmes are often referred to as 'taught' or 'professional' doctorates, and they normally take three years of full-time study.

Taught doctorate for professional practice

If you want to practise in some professions, the qualifying route is by professional doctorate, e.g. Clinical Psychology or Educational and Child Psychology. So if you want be a Clinical or Educational Psychologist, you will have to complete a professional doctorate. Again, these normally take three years of full-time study.

brilliant definition

Doctoral-level degrees can be research-based, taught or a combination of both. Those with a substantial taught element are professional doctorates. Some professions demand a taught doctorate in order to be included on the register and practise in that profession.

Where and how to study

Full-time or part-time?

You can see that there are several different types of postgraduate programmes to choose from. They can be offered in two attendance modes: full-time and part-time. Any course will have a mixture of teaching delivery and self-directed learning. Full-time courses might require attendance most days of the week or only a couple of days. This often depends on the nature of the subject studied: Engineering and Science degrees need you to put a lot of time into laboratory work, which obviously can only be done in the university. Art and Design courses also demand long hours in the studio, which could be done at home but is more likely to be done on campus. You will need to check with individual courses how much attendance is required; you can't assume that all full-time courses have the same classroom hours. Courses that lead to professional qualification will require practice or placement hours that can take up several weeks each semester. So the decision to study full-time might be made for you if the programme you want is only offered in full-time mode. Once you start to look at the courses on offer, you'll get a feel for what can be studied flexibly and what must be studied full-time.

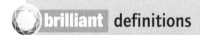 **definitions**

Full-time study normally expects attendance on several days each week, with significant self-directed study.

Part-time study might involve only one day of teaching per week, along with self-directed work to be undertaken by you during the week.

On campus, at a distance or online?

There are also three recognised ways of teaching a programme, sometimes called 'modes of delivery'. They are: campus-based, distance-learning or online learning. You may already be familiar with these distinctions from your undergraduate course.

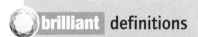 definitions

Campus programmes are based at the university. You will meet your lecturers and tutors face to face and they will deliver lectures in person.

Distance learning programmes do not necessarily involve any attendance at university. Teaching is delivered through module guides or study handbooks, which can be in print or accessible online. Tutorials are delivered by email, phone or online.

Online programmes make extensive use of information communication technology for teaching and learning. These include: virtual learning environments; online teaching materials; video and podcasts; discussion boards; wikis; facilitated chatrooms, and forums. Tutorials are delivered by: email; phone; video conference, or skype.

Blurring distinct modes of study

These clear distinctions do get blurred in practice, particularly as developments in new technology and mobile communication make it ever easier to pick up online materials. It is true that a student on an online programme might never set foot on campus, but it is equally entirely possible that they do visit from time to time and might arrange to meet a tutor if that is mutually convenient. By the same token, a student studying on campus may well pick up a pod or videocast of a lecture, or access online teaching and learning materials in a virtual learning environment. It can also be a really interesting peer learning experience to invite a mix of students (online, distance, part- and full-time) to participate in a facilitated online chat, or to contribute to a discussion forum, as this can lead to a powerful mix of experience and insight.

 tip

Lecturers are making greater use of mixed media. Even if you're an on-campus student, check out online material for your modules, e.g. podcasts or films posted by your tutors.

Study in the United Kingdom or venture abroad?

Postgraduate study abroad

You might already be thinking about doing your second degree at a different university, but what about doing it in a different country? You will of course need to work through all the issues around postgraduate study that are in this chapter. However, it is worth mentioning here the possibility of studying abroad for your second degree. You are probably more confident now than you were when you started your undergraduate course, so you might be prepared to widen your horizons at this stage.

▶ brilliant example

'Biological Psychology opened my eyes to a world of scientific knowledge and curiosity. To my delight, this course integrated aspects of Comparative Psychology focusing on the behaviour of non-human primates. This inspired my final-year research project, studying the self-directed behaviour of chimpanzees at Chester Zoo. In 2008, I continued my studies at Bucknell University in the USA to study for my Masters degree in Psychology, where I studied the behaviour of squirrel monkeys for my graduate thesis. After a two-year exceedingly rigorous programme and adjusting to some differences between the British and American education systems, I recently graduated with my MSc degree.'

Sam, BSc (Hons) Psychology, MSc

Language of instruction can be English, even in Europe

You would normally be expected to have sufficient fluency in the language of instruction (i.e. the language in which the postgraduate course is taught and examined) before you are admitted onto a study programme. However, if your language levels are not yet sufficient to cope with postgraduate study, you can follow our brilliant example of someone studying in the United States, where the language of instruction was no problem.

Even across Europe, you can find a way across the language barrier because many postgraduate programmes are offered in English. This is particularly so where the programme wants to attract a range of students of different nationalities, which means English can be used as the common language. Examples of this would include the Master of Business Administration (MBA) offered at the Copenhagen Business School in Denmark, or at the University of Oulu in northern Finland. Doctoral-level programmes are also offered in English medium, e.g. PhD Chemistry and Materials Technology at the Tomas Bata University in the Czech Republic or PhD in Astronomy at the University of Porto in Portugal. Even if your foreign language level is modest at the start of a postgraduate programme, by virtue of living overseas, you will have plenty of chance to develop it. Choosing to study abroad would also help you develop a wider perspective, which could be of interest to employers when you look for work. Take a look at Chapter 5 'The global graduate: travel and employability' for more on this.

Increasingly, employers will look for some more interesting skills: things like cultural sensitivity and what makes a global graduate.

Carl Gilleard, Chief Executive, Association of Graduate Recruiters

Why study beyond an undergraduate degree?

It is important to ask yourself why you are even thinking of continuing your studies beyond an undergraduate degree, and it is highly likely that many other people will be asking you that very question: fellow students; family; friends; possibly your bank manager or any potential funding body; and perhaps, most critically, the admissions tutor for the programme you want to go onto.

There are many possible responses to the basic question: why study at a higher level? Each one takes a slightly different perspective, so you don't need to respond positively to all of them, but you do need to respond positively to at least one.

Because you really enjoy your subject

Intellectual curiosity and deep enjoyment of your subject are both important drivers if you are thinking of an academic degree. If you are thinking of a research degree, either MPhil initially or PhD eventually, they are both absolutely essential. On a research degree, you are going to study one small aspect of one specialist area of one discipline. Just look back at our brilliant example: Sam studied Psychology, took an option in Biological Psychology, which narrowed into Comparative Psychology and focused on non-human primates, which led her to work on the behaviour of squirrel monkeys. Once you have narrowed your own focus to your own research inquiry, you are then going to work for 12 months solid at the very least to reach Masters level. If you continue to PhD, you will be working on it for another two years full-time, and perhaps for several years if you study part-time. Your interest is what will pull you through, month after month, perhaps year after year. If you just feel very strongly that you want to delve further into your specialist area, don't worry if this seems irrational: it's probably a good sign.

brilliant example

'My ambition for the future is to complete my doctorate – something I hope to be embarking on in the very near future. Long term – who knows? I have been trained as a therapeutic practitioner and use a narrative therapy approach in much of my work. I hope to publish, to continue developing this way of working and to reflect on my practice as much as possible. I might end up in a lecture theatre near you!! Whichever way, I hope very much to be developing my personal practice in psychology until I retire. Psychology for me has been one of the most amazing and life-changing subjects to study. I have been studying it for seven to eight years and still it is ever changing, moving and posing me constant questions. I could not ask for more.'

Rhona, BSc (Hons) Psychology, PGCE, MSc

Because it's the main route to a career as either lecturer or researcher

If you are drawn to a career as a lecturer in higher education or a researcher, you will need to get a doctoral-level qualification, probably a PhD. There are some exceptions to this, but they really are the exceptions to the rule. Most universities now, when advertising for a lecturer or researcher post, will expect you either to have been awarded your doctorate or to be very far advanced, with perhaps only weeks to go before you formally complete your doctoral degree. This doesn't necessarily mean that you have to go straight from being at school to being an undergraduate to being a doctoral student to being a lecturer. You might undertake doctoral study as a mature student, perhaps even part-time while you are working. This is by no means unusual and would not be viewed adversely by selection panels. But you will still need to secure the doctorate in order to secure a sustainable career in higher education.

 **brilliant** example

'I now work in academic support as a research and development officer, having completed an MSc in Mathematics. My role utilises the statistical knowledge I gained on my course for evaluative research. I also use the IT knowledge I gained on my course, to support the work of the department. I have recently begun a PhD and I hope eventually to use my knowledge and experience to become a lecturer in higher education.'

Nicola, BSc (Hons) Mathematics with Computer Science and Information Systems, MSc Mathematics

Because entry to a profession demands an M-level qualification

Some jobs, particularly professional jobs, demand a postgraduate qualification. These professional (sometimes called vocational) courses are awarded by universities, but can also be recognised by professional bodies. Professional bodies set standards and regulate practitioners.

Examples include the Institute of Civil Engineers or the Chartered Society of Physiotherapy. So you are awarded a postgraduate degree which can also give you access to a profession and licence to practise as a named professional. It is important to check (with the professional body) whether you need to have a recognised qualification, and then to check (with the university) whether the course you want has got professional body accreditation.

Thomas, our next brilliant example, completed a law degree and did a relevant academic Masters programme before undertaking the course required by the professional body as the first part of training to be a barrister.

▶ brilliant example

'After completing my degree, I decided to continue my studies in order to give me a more specialised knowledge. So I completed a Masters degree in Law, Medicine and Healthcare. Completing the Masters degree has provided me with more in-depth knowledge on a subject which I enjoy and ultimately wish to practise in.

Following my Masters degree, I completed the Bar Professional Training course. I found the course extremely interesting as I was using the legal knowledge gained from my degrees in a practical context.'

Thomas, LLB, LLM

Because M-level qualifications give you leverage in the labour market

You'll realise by now that we use 'leverage' to mean gaining the necessary skills and know-how that enable you to move to a better job. Taking a Masters-level qualification can be the transition from one occupation to another. This can be within the same occupational sector, but extending your professional repertoire, e.g. an architect taking a course in Renewable Energy in the Built Environment. This can be to facilitate a move between two related occupational sectors, e.g. from mental health nursing to psychoanalyst. Or it can be a career change to something completely different, e.g. from laboratory technician to librarian. The training might be a requirement to practise in the new occupation, or it might help to formalise a particular interest within your own professional domain, as this example shows.

▶ brilliant example

'After completing my BSc Honours degree in Sports and Exercise Science, I started my full-time career in the fitness industry and worked my way up to achieve a position in the NHS as a physical activity advisor . . . my personal ambition was to enhance my knowledge and expertise around cardiovascular disease, treatment, therapy and post-rehabilitation. I decided that, despite working full-time, I wanted to continue my studying career and found the MSc was ideal . . . I have continued to work with the regional cardiac rehabilitation service, and have found that postgraduate qualifications not only give you the opportunity to boost your knowledge but give you that edge to show you are a committed individual who is willing to work hard.'

Jennifer, MSc Cardiovascular Rehabilitation

Because you can develop specialist know-how for niche sectors

You can use a Masters degree not only as an academic qualification, but also as a time-limited space in which you will develop know-how that will put you in a better position for getting into very specialist or niche sectors. Some Masters programmes, particularly in the creative industries, will build in a lot of time for you to develop your own professional repertoire: some creative writing programmes, for example. On many specialist Masters, the university lecturers will make great efforts to bring in specialist lecturers from the relevant industry. Indeed, your lecturers themselves may well be practising in their industry. So, as well as extending your knowledge and understanding, you are given privileged access to valuable contacts within your chosen field. You need to be proactive here. Access and opportunities are very much the start of the story. It is up to you to seize chances and do everything you can to make the most of them. Networking is particularly important here, so have a look at Chapter 1 'Accessing job opportunities', which gives you practical help on how to network.

▶ brilliant example

'During my second year studying Civil Engineering I started to realise I had doubts about whether Civil Engineering would be right for me. I wondered if it might be possible to transfer the engineering skills I was gaining to another part of the industry . . . motorsport. I realised I would need a more relevant degree to appeal to potential employers (in motorsport). I also thought it crucial to finish my Masters in Civil Engineering . . . in case I need to fall back on it . . . The Motorsport Engineering MSc was the only specialist qualification available in the UK at that time, with strong links to the motorsport sector. If I was to get a career as an engineer in motorsport, I felt I had to get on it! It has taken a great deal of determination, but now I am a systems engineer in a Formula One racing team.'

Oliver, MEng Civil Engineering, MSc Motorsport Engineering and Management

Because now is a good time

We have seen that you don't need to take a Masters qualification immediately on completion of your first degree, and we already know that not everyone starts an undergraduate career immediately after leaving school, so M-level qualifications can be taken at any stage in your career or, indeed, at any stage in your life.

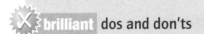 **dos and don'ts**

Do undertake postgraduate study because

✔ you're passionate about your subject;

✔ you want to gain access to a profession;

✔ you want to progress in your sector;

✔ you want to move into a new sector;

✔ you are at a point in your life where you have time.

Don't undertake postgraduate study because

✘ you've no idea what else to do;

✘ you want to put off starting your career;

✘ your mates are doing it;

✘ your tutors think your talents would be wasted on the job market.

How to choose the right course for you

Be clear about why you want to study beyond an undergraduate degree

The earlier section in this chapter has explained that postgraduate degrees can meet a range of different demands: to satisfy intellectual curiosity; to satisfy professional body requirements; to help you break into a niche sector; or to prepare you for a career in higher education. Once you have clarified what it is you want to get out of postgraduate study, you can focus your search on the appropriate type of course.

Work out where you want to do your postgraduate study

Do you have a free choice of where you want to study? Perhaps you are constrained in terms of location, because of family commitments or housing arrangements. Before you restrict your search to a very limited geographical area, look at online or distance programmes. Or check out just how much attendance is required on campus: could you manage to stay overnight just for the study days?

If you do have the luxury of free choice, make the most of it! When compared to other segments of the labour force, graduates are more likely to move around for their jobs and graduate employers are more likely to expect them to relocate. So now is your chance to try living in another place or even another country.

How to find out more

Look at what individual universities offer

There are lots of postgraduate courses on offer, and lots of help in accessing information about them. There is plenty of online material: universities will have websites and, certainly within England, Wales and Northern Ireland, they are expected to publish clear and fairly detailed information about their courses, often called a specification. You can also request printed prospectuses from universities you are interested in: they often produce a separate postgraduate version which is less bulky than the undergraduate version. If you're not sure where to start, the postgraduate study section of the Graduate Prospects website (**www.prospects.ac.uk**) lets you search by region and subject.

Look at professional body course listings

If you are applying for a professional or vocational programme, you can turn to the relevant professional body to check what university courses offer accredited programmes. This can really help to focus your search.

Look beyond the UK

If you are thinking of studying outside the UK but in the European Union, don't be put off by the breathtaking amount of choice on offer. There are some very nifty websites with useful search facilities that allow you to set clear parameters for your search. The studyportals site **www.masterspor-tal.eu** is useful because it includes different sections on Masters, PhDs and scholarships, but is limited to Europe. There is a whole world out there beyond the EU, so look online for them too.

Probe beneath the glossy brochure

Ask people what they think: tutors, postgraduates, online contacts

Obviously, universities want to attract the best talent, so the course information they publish shows things in the best possible light. You can probe beneath the surface by asking people what they really think. Your tutors may have a view, so ask them about a programme's reputation. What do they think of the people who teach on the course? If your tutors are themselves qualified professionals, what advice would they give about where to study? Do what we did, and ask people who have undertaken postgraduate programmes. You can start this in your own department by finding out who the postgrads are and asking them about their courses. (Don't worry, they don't usually bite!) You can also make use of social networking sites to post questions and learn from other people's experience. See Chapter 1 'Accessing job opportunities' if you need help getting started on social networking sites.

Go and visit

As you may know from your undergraduate experience, universities run open days where you meet students and tutors from the courses on offer, and have a look at the facilities. One of the very best things about physically going to a university open day is that you get a feel for it. So it may be a bit inconvenient, and it may cost you money to get there, but going to an open day is always worth it. Even if you come away convinced it is not the right course or location for you, you are better informed, which is definite progress in your decision making, even if it doesn't feel like it at the time.

Of course, it may not be practical for you to visit the campus, especially if it is overseas. You can still interact with students there, but online rather than in person. See if there is a webcam or a 360-degree tour. Or maybe you could Skype someone there to get a feel for the location.

 **tips**

Questions to ask:

- What kind of jobs did last year's completers go on to?

- Do you have any links with the industry/profession?

- How much time will I spend in lectures and tutorials?

- How much self-directed study should I expect to do?

- What makes this course different from others?

- What kind of specialist teaching space do you offer?

What kind of a student am I?

As well as asking course tutors and postgraduate students some probing questions, you also need to ask yourself some probing questions too. While there are different types of postgraduate courses on offer, there are also different types of postgraduate student. You are, of course, a complex human being, and to pin you down by asking only a couple of questions is only to scratch the surface of what makes you the unique individual you are. However, thinking about two fairly basic behaviours can help you to interrogate whether a particular course mode is right for you. So just try to answer these two questions:

Are you (a) self-disciplined in your study or (b) more easily diverted?

Are you (a) happy in your own company or (b) do you seek out the company of others?

If you are opting for the (b) answers, maybe you shouldn't be opting for a distance-learning programme where you will have to structure your own study timetable, and will be working alone for the vast majority of your time. You know yourself better than anybody, so make use of that self-knowledge to identify the kind of course that will allow you to do your best.

Funding postgraduate study

You will realise very quickly that one stark difference between funding your postgraduate study, compared with funding your undergraduate degree, is that there isn't a unified system for funding that you just slot into. The sources of funding are out there, and there is good signposting.

People who can advise you

Tutors on your undergraduate programme can be helpful; remember that they probably had to go through the same process themselves. Admissions tutors on postgraduate courses are also a very good source of information and, as it is in their interests to get funded students on their courses, they are likely to be helpful.

Grants, loans and bursaries

Funding can be in the form of grants, bursaries or loans. Grants and bursaries are where the money is given to you and you don't need to pay it back. You will, however, have to satisfy the conditions attached to the grant: if the grant expects you to complete the postgraduate course successfully, you'll need to do just that. Loans, however, do need to be repaid and the repayments will be with interest, so you end up paying back more than the amount you borrowed. Graduate Prospects produces an annual guide to postgraduate funding which comes out in September. This is an invaluable starting point, and you would do well to pick up your free copy from your university careers service at the very start of the academic year *before* the year you hope to start your postgraduate course.

brilliant timesaver

Get hold of the Graduate Prospects annual publication: *The Postgraduate Funding Guide*. Published in September, free copies should be available at your university careers service. Failing that, buy your own copy online.

Funding yourself: combining study with employment

All of these sources of advice will merely signpost you; it is very much up to you to track down sources and follow up leads and, if you don't do it, it is unlikely that anybody else will do it for you. This section will outline all the sources of funding that might be open to you. A further alternative is to fund yourself, perhaps by mixing part-time study with part-time work. Official statistics show that about half of postgraduate students do this. The problem here being that you will need to find the balance between these two competing demands on your time and brain power. One good way forward is to find employment that enhances your area of study, for example working as a lab or teaching assistant if you are doing doctoral study, or doing sessional youth work if you are studying youth work.

Be resilient and resourceful

For most people, accommodation is their biggest single expenditure. Rather than looking for sufficient funding to pay rent, could you find some way of getting a rent reduction or even a job with accommodation? Perhaps you could be a warden in a university hall of residence if you are a postgraduate student, or maybe you could ask family or friends to let you have a room rent free in exchange for helping around the house. The chances are that you will end up stitching together a patchwork of funding to get you through. Resilience and resourcefulness come into play when funding postgraduate study. If you find you are getting disheartened, remember that many people before you have somehow found a way, and so can you.

Sources of funding for postgraduate study

Universities themselves fund postgraduates

You may be surprised to find that universities themselves sometimes offer funding direct to postgraduate students. Often this comes about because the course tutor (or someone in the university administration) has secured funding (from public money or from employers) to meet the demand for training or research. This is more likely to be limited to designated programmes, rather than applying to the individual student irrespective of the course chosen. There might be a brilliant fit between the course you want to do and the courses that are funded. Or you might be thinking about modifying your course choice in order to follow the funding. That's fine, but do think this one through so you are confident you have the enthusiasm and ability you will need in order to succeed on the funded course, rather than your original choice.

Research councils

A small part of the work of research councils is to fund postgraduate students through grants. There are seven research councils in total: Arts and Humanities Research Council; Biotechnology and Biological Sciences Research Council; Economic and Social Research Council; Engineering and Physical Sciences Research Council; Medical Research Council; Natural Environment Research Council; and Science and Technology Facilities Council. The big advantage of research council funding is that it is a grant rather than a loan, and it should be enough for you to pay course fees and live on, albeit modestly. The funding can be for either a Masters degree or doctoral study, and successful applicants would normally have a good first degree, that is either a first class or upper second class honours degree. Eligibility is usually restricted to UK or EU nationals. You need to be aware that competition is intense: research council funding is keenly sought and hard won.

Public funding

You might be eligible for public funding outside the research councils. For example, students in Northern Ireland and in Scotland can apply to particular schemes for postgraduate funding, and the European Union is another source worth considering. As eligibility criteria are different for each funding stream, and can also change from year to year (particularly when there is pressure on public funding in general), you will need to pick your way through the details of each of the various funding streams to find one that could work for you.

Commercial loans

A loan must of course be repaid, and commercial loans will need to be repaid with interest. There is one high street bank (NatWest) which offers a commercial loan specifically targeted to postgraduate training. Broadly speaking, it is restricted to full-time postgraduate courses which lead to a professional qualification. They also run a loan scheme for MBA courses.

Professional and career development loans (PCDL) are available for a wider range of courses, provided that they lead to a trade, occupation or profession. The course can be full or part-time, or by distance learning, and can last for up to two years. While you are on the course, the interest on your loan is paid by the Young People's Learning Agency. You have to start paying the loan back one month after you complete your course, through a repayment plan agreed with one of the three high street banks involved in the scheme.

brilliant tip

Check out what loans are currently on offer. Banks can withdraw or launch new products, and schemes using public money can be subject to change of government policy.

Charities

Charities vary enormously in scale and scope, so some will offer big grants to cover tuition fees and living costs for full-time postgraduate study, where others will make only a modest contribution to your overall needs. On the principle that any money is better than no money, even the modest sums are worth applying for. Each funding scheme and every different charity will have its own procedures. They are, however, all likely to set clear eligibility criteria and to have a set procedure for funding applications. All of this will take time, so applying in the September of your final undergraduate year will not be too soon. You need to be aware that some charities will award a grant only once they are satisfied that you have exhausted all other possible sources of funding, so you'll need to show that you have made applications to some of the other funding streams outlined here as well as applying for charitable funds.

Employers can sometimes be persuaded

If you are already employed, perhaps in a graduate job, it is worth looking to your employer for funding. There may already be a company scheme in place, in which case you'll need to check out eligibility and application procedure. If it is a big company, the human resources department should be able to advise here. If it is a small to medium-sized enterprise (SME) it is worth having a look at government or EU funding for workplace development. If there is nothing like this already in place, it is still worth exploring this option with your employer, but you will probably have to make a proposal. Think about this from the employer's side: what's in it for them? How will you be able to add value to the company once you have the postgraduate qualification? Could the postgraduate study itself be of value to the company – for example if you are doing some kind of research, could this help the company be more productive or competitive? Even if the company can't pay all your fees, could they make a contribution, or could you share the cost between you? Or could they pay the fees up front with you paying them back through salary sacrifice, a bit like an interest free season ticket loan? Although it may seem daunting to approach your employer for help with funding your career progression, the very fact that you are taking the initiative says a lot about you as an employee: it shows you are resourceful, proactive and business-minded. So, prepare your case well and go for it.

Which comes first – getting a place or getting funding?

Clearly, there are two key challenges that you face as an aspiring postgraduate: you need to secure a place on the course of your choice, and you need to secure the funding that will enable you to take up the place and succeed on the course. Don't worry about getting a place before you get funding, or indeed getting funding before you get a place. Certainly don't get so stuck worrying about doing things in the wrong order that you don't actually take any action. Pursue these twin challenges at the same time. The worst thing that can happen is that you end up with more than one source of funding and more than one offer of a place. That's quite an enviable position to be in, so risk it.

 **tip**

Don't worry about the sequence of securing a place on a course and securing funding. Pursue both at the same time: you'll probably need to apply to more than one course, and you'll probably need to consider more than one source of funding. Just get started with both challenges.

Making a good application

Everything that applies to job applications applies to applications for postgraduate courses. Chapter 10 takes you through this in more detail, but here are a few key pointers to get you started.

Dates and deadlines

Some postgraduate courses run to strict deadlines by which applications must be received. You need to check if this applies to your chosen programme and, if it does, you must be sure to get your application in on time or it simply will not be considered. You'll need to give yourself enough time to work through your application so you don't have to rush to meet the deadline.

Even if programmes don't publish a deadline, if an admissions tutor has received sufficient good applicants to fill the available spaces, they may well stop making offers (conditional or unconditional) and start a waiting list. This means you'll get a place on the course only if someone who is holding an offer of a place turns it down. So it is better to apply early than to risk the course filling up without you.

Personal statement

Make sure that your personal statement shows that you have got what they are looking for: go back to the course literature and see what they say about the kind of student they want. You will need to show motivation, ideally by including examples of how that motivation has shown through already. You will also need to show ability to study at postgraduate level:

this includes the ability to write effectively, so take care to structure your work and to check spelling and grammar are correct.

Referees

You will need to provide references. For postgraduate courses, it is usual to request two referees, both of them academic. You will need to talk to your referees and get their agreement before you include their names on your application. You need to be clear with them that this is an academic reference, which means you are going to need to approach people who can actually comment on your academic ability. This might be your personal tutor, a tutor from your first couple of years' study, or your final-year dissertation supervisor, but should include someone who is familiar with your academic record right now. If it has been a while since you have been studying, this can be difficult. However, you will need to try to find someone who can comment on your ability. This might mean going back to your last place of study, even if that is some time ago. Or you could use someone more recent, but they will need to say something about your potential for postgraduate study based on their observation and judgement. It is helpful here if your referee has personal experience of postgraduate study, so they can use their understanding of what postgraduate study demands to inform their judgement of your potential to achieve a postgraduate degree.

brilliant tip

Make sure you have two academic referees. Both should be able to comment on your potential to achieve a postgraduate degree. If you have been out of study for a long time so can't readily locate an academic referee, try to find someone who has personal experience of studying at postgraduate level, even if they are not a tutor.

Applying even if you don't have a first degree

You don't necessarily need to have a first (undergraduate) degree in order to be accepted onto a postgraduate course. Vocational degrees have a long and noble tradition of taking on people with relevant work experience. However, in addition to that experience, you will need to show that you have the capacity to achieve at a higher level of study. So it is important to showcase any steps you have taken to increase your knowledge and know-how in the field of study. This may have been practical experience, but may also have been through work-shadowing a professional, or doing some work experience or volunteering in the field. Your written work will be very important in making a first impression, so do spend time on your application form and get someone to have a look at it and give you constructive feedback. That can be nerve-racking, but better to get feedback from someone so you can improve it before you send the application off unchecked and not even get invited to interview for a place on the course.

Applying without a 'good' degree

A 'good' degree means a first class or upper second class honours degree. Research degrees normally demand a good degree as a minimum for entry. Whilst it is possible to be offered a place on a research degree without a good first degree, it is very unusual. Don't despair if you can't go immediately from undergraduate to research degree because of this hurdle. You can go step by step; by progressing from undergraduate to postgraduate degree and from there to doctoral-level study. It takes longer, but that time allows you to develop your scholarly performance, which will stay with you for the rest of your learning days, so it is never time wasted.

Applying to jobs once you have your postgraduate qualification

If everything goes right, you'll get a place on the postgraduate course you want, and you'll make a brilliant success of it. And, before you know it, you'll be making applications yet again, this time for a job. Present your postgraduate studies as a thought-through career choice, not the result of procrastination, or a reluctance to enter the world of work. Check back through earlier parts of this chapter for good, positive reasons for choosing postgraduate study. Show the employer very clearly what you yourself have gained through your postgraduate study. It should have enhanced your skillset and mindset (if that means nothing to you, have a look at Chapter 2) and so you are offering added value to the employer. Be confident: you have travelled further for having undertaken higher-level study.

 **recap**

- Make sure you have a positive reason for going on to postgraduate study.

- Choose a course that plays to your personal strengths and circumstances.

- Consider studying outside the UK.

- Don't worry in what order to apply for a place and to apply for funding: the important thing is to apply early.

- Be resourceful and resilient in funding your postgraduate study.

- You'll need an academic reference, so talk to your tutor about your plans.

- Be positive in selling your postgraduate qualification to an employer; it should add value to you both.

What to do next

If you do nothing else, get hold of the Graduate Prospects publications about postgraduate study and read through them for ideas. See if there is a postgraduate fair or open day either at your current or target university: register for it and go there to get a feel for what's on offer. Talk to your personal tutor (or a tutor whose judgement you trust) about your plans. See if there are current postgraduates in your department who you can talk to about their experiences.

PART 2

How to make the most of what's out there

CHAPTER 7

Knowing who you are: skills, interests and values

There are two important perspectives when planning your brilliant career. One is what's out there, which we explored in Chapter 1; the other is who you are, which we cover in this chapter. It's good to try and have both of these perspectives in your mind. Both have enormous value – a sound knowledge of graduate opportunities helps you to be realistic in your plans, while an understanding of your own strengths and preferences will make you a more successful applicant. Even more importantly, this understanding and its application to your career plan will make you a more fulfilled person. When jobs are scarce it's easy to focus on getting whatever is available – and certainly it may be necessary to compromise or to plan for the longer term – but even in a restricted job market there is still scope for choice.

Skills, interests and values

In this chapter we will help you to analyse your own skills, interests and values.

Here are three fundamental questions: spend a little time thinking about them, making a note of your answers – just words or phrases will be fine. We are giving you some prompts to help.

What are you good at?

Think about:

- technical skills associated with your degree subject, such as using specialist equipment or software;

- generic or transferable work skills, such as cash handling, working under pressure, meeting targets, supervising others, report writing;

- soft skills, such as working in a team, communication, time management, showing initiative.

What are you interested in?

This question covers the kind of physical and social setting you want to work in (office-based, a variety of locations, outdoors, production, laboratory, in a team or alone) as well as the subject matter – would you like to use your degree subject in your job? Remember that around half of graduate jobs don't specify a particular subject, so, while it's not necessary for you to use your subject, it might be something you would like to do.

What do you believe in and how does this fit with your career plan?

At first sight this is less straightforward than the other two questions. To help you, think about which of the following is something you care about:

- protecting the environment;

- improving the life chances of people who are disadvantaged;

- contributing to the economy through provision of goods or services;

- being creative, with words or materials;

- sharing, creating or discovering knowledge;

- achieving a high standard of living.

These are examples of values, or beliefs that guide the way we live our lives. Some people live out their values outside their working life, for example a high-flying business executive whose work role is to contribute to the economy and who gives time and money to a local charity for the homeless; others look for a working life that is consistent with their values, for example an international development worker. Thinking about what matters to you is another way to identify suitable job opportunities.

Make a note of your answers to our three questions.

 **tip**

Think about these three questions:

- What are you good at?
- What are you interested in?
- What do you believe in and how does this fit with your career plan?

Why does it matter?

Firstly, knowing yourself better helps you to get started if you have no particular preferences about your future career. If you can think and learn about what you are good at, what you are interested in, and what you believe in, you will begin to identify job choices. You will also be able to eliminate jobs from your career plan and this is just as useful, as it helps you to narrow down the possibilities. It also helps you to identify the underlying factors in the jobs you are both choosing and eliminating, which in turn helps you to broaden your range of choices. As you learn more about the detail of job opportunities you will be able to fit this knowledge with what you know about yourself. Remember to refer back to Part 1 of this book to revisit the kinds of opportunities open to you as a graduate.

Secondly, career success and satisfaction are more likely to be achieved if there is a good match with what you are good at, what you are interested in, and what you believe in and believe to be important. Have a look at this brilliant example to see what we mean.

▶ brilliant example

'There was so much that my course taught me, including skills that I can use in all aspects of my life. Doing Drama and Theatre Studies encouraged me to be myself and show the world what I had to offer, and this began opening up so many opportunities for me. As well as the content of the course, I developed skills like working to deadlines and self-organisation, which brought with it self-discipline and an increase in my independence. I feel that all these skills have stood me in good stead for the world of work.

Using the wealth of experience I gained at university, along with the academic knowledge, I am now working as an Arts & Cultural Positive Activities Officer for an amazing community interest company delivering activities to children in deprived areas. Workshops range from DJ-ing through drama and graffiti to film production, to raise the aspirations of young people in those communities. The children have the opportunity to work towards an arts award, a nationally recognised certificate which boosts their confidence and gives them something to be proud of. I thoroughly enjoy this role and the satisfaction it gives me in seeing young people, who once may not have had many aspirations, achieve and build in their confidence and outlook on life.'

Joanne, BA (Hons) Drama and Theatre Studies

Now read this example again and look for evidence of Joanne's skills, interests and values in her story. All three are critical to her success in, and enjoyment of, her brilliant graduate career.

We noticed her references to:

- working to deadlines;
- self-organisation;
- self-discipline;
- increased independence;
- satisfaction at seeing young people with low aspirations grow in confidence and broaden their outlook;
- her interest in using her degree subject.

Each of us is unique

Although we referred to Joanne's achieving a good match between her own skills, interests and values and the job she has chosen, this doesn't mean that we are trying to put square pegs in round holes. Two students on the same course, getting the same grades, doing the same kind of part-time work, will each make their own unique and valid sense of their experience – which in turn will impact on their career planning. A skilled careers adviser will help you to 'make meaning' of your own particular experiences and ambitions. So, in addition to considering your skills, interests and values and how these might be fulfilled in particular job roles, you might also think about key turning points in your life so far, how people or events have influenced you, and the extent to which you take a logical, rational approach or an intuitive approach to planning your future. These are all factors that contribute to your uniqueness.

The skill of reflection

To understand more about your skills, interests and values you need to develop your personal insight and self-awareness. Some people are comfortable describing what they think, feel and believe, others less so – it might not have been encouraged in their upbringing, or they might not find it easy to put such concepts into words. It often takes someone else to tell us what we are good at – perhaps we fear sounding big-headed or overconfident. As far as interests and values are concerned, we might need help in generalising from the specific example to the broader category – 'I really enjoy the voluntary work I'm doing and believe it is making a difference, but I don't know of any paid jobs like this.' Tests, questionnaires and inventories are a great help in learning more about ourselves and we will come to these later. But first let's look at what we can learn just by taking time to reflect on what has happened.

How reflection works

Watch any post-match discussion of a big football game and you will see the experts taking the game apart, reviewing the successes as well as the weak points of the game and analysing the performance of every player in great detail. If you are a football fan, you might well have evaluated the game in the same way. If not, you might be amazed at the perception of the experts, at the extent to which they notice and interpret what's going on in the game. We can be sure that the manager, coach and players use the same process of review soon after the match, in order to make improvements for next time. What has this got to do with career planning?

- Firstly, the experts and professionals take time to reflect.
- Secondly, they know what they are looking for and can describe what they see.
- Thirdly, they know what this means for future performance.

So let's apply this to something you might do, say working in a group of other students to complete a project. You get an average mark for the work. Which of the following do you do?

1 Say, 'Great, that's a pass', and think no more about it.
2 Take time to read your feedback, talk to your tutor, think about what went well and why, what went badly and why, what your own role was in the group, how you could behave differently next time to get a better result, and then make a note somewhere to remind you.

Option 2 might sound like a lot of trouble – but the gain is that you will have an insight into how you work as a member of a team (a classic area for you to cover in an application and for employers to explore at interview) and a sense of how to become more skilled. You will also find that, if you get into this way of thinking, it will become part of your behaviour and much less of an effort. Your university may have an electronic framework, or e-portfolio, to help you to keep your record. Otherwise, just devise a simple template that you can update as significant events occur.

Try this yourself

Now try this one for yourself, this time focusing on your communication skills. Take an example – giving a presentation to your seminar group or handling a difficult customer in the workplace – and answer the following questions.

1 What happened? (Describe the setting and the activity/incident.)

2 What went well? Why? How do you know?

3 What went less well? Why? How do you know?

4 What would you do differently next time? What do you need to help you to do this?

Notice that there is a new question here – how do you know? The answers to this question are the evidence you need to show that you have the skill in question. Employers will seek evidence – it's not enough to say, 'I'm really good at communicating with people.'

Where's the evidence?

Let's go back to the example of giving a presentation. Evidence can come from:

- your own self-reflection ('although I covered the ground, I was running out of time and I felt as if I rushed the last part');

- the response of the audience (they looked interested/stayed awake/asked questions/told me afterwards they understood it); and

- feedback from your tutor (informal comments, written feedback, an actual grade or mark).

Gathering this evidence and being willing to listen to feedback will make a real difference to what you do next time – in other words, it will improve your performance.

So go back to those four steps – what happened, what went well, what went less well, what will you do differently next time and try to apply them. You will learn more about your own skills, and you will get better. Best of all you will develop a skill employers really value, because you will be a person who learns from experience and who actively seeks opportunities for learning.

> Most graduates now are expected to do regular evaluations of where they are at and where they are going . . . developing the individual to the point where they can take control of their life, their learning and their career.
>
> Carl Gilleard, Chief Executive, Association of Graduate Recruiters

More techniques to help you to know who you are

Let's go back to those three questions at the start of the chapter:

- What are you good at?
- What are you interested in?
- What do you believe in and how does this fit with your career plan?

For some people, thinking about their skills, interests and values is enough, especially if they have developed the skill of reflection we discussed earlier in the chapter. However, many people need some help in structuring their thoughts, from talking to someone, e.g. a careers adviser, to completing a questionnaire.

Talk to people

If your university offers one-to-one careers consultations, you really don't need to know what you want to do before you book your slot! Careers advisers use skilful questioning to guide you through these three areas as a way to help you to develop a career plan. It's surprising how often 'I don't know what I want to do' really means 'I've got a few ideas but I'm not sure . . .'

If you can't get access to one-to-one consultations with a careers adviser, talk to your personal tutor, or a tutor you get on with who knows you well. Just thinking aloud with a good listener can move you forward. Also, try other people you know who might have some time – friends, family, someone you know through a part-time job or work experience. Get them to help you to answer our three questions. If they are in a position to give you feedback, ask them, so that you get a better insight into your skills.

brilliant example

'With an idea in mind of the type of career I was interested in, I visited the university careers service to talk to a careers adviser about my options. With the use of interactive software I was able to analyse my skills and get possible career ideas which I was then able to discuss with the careers adviser. She also referred me to a really good website, Graduate Prospects, which contained a wealth of different information for me to research. I found all these processes really useful and realised that my strengths were in communication and teamworking, and that I enjoyed a competitive environment.'

Paul, BSc (Hons) Sport and Exercise Science

Use psychometric tests

In Chapter 11 of this book we will be looking at how tests and questionnaires are used by employers during selection. In this chapter we will tell you how to use them to learn more about yourself. Tests used in career planning or selection are often referred to as 'psychometric' tests. This simply means tests that 'measure the mind'. We will look more at the detail of psychometric tests in Chapter 11; for now, here are some quick definitions.

brilliant definitions

Psychometric test – a set of questions that measure an aspect of mental performance or behaviour. The word psychometric means measuring the mind.

Aptitude test – a measure of a particular aptitude or ability consisting of questions with right and wrong answers. Scores are compared with others to assess performance.

Personality test – a set of questions designed to explore and describe aspects of personality, or what kind of person we are. There are no right or wrong answers, though when employers use a personality test they may be looking for certain characteristics.

You can use aptitude tests to check out your ability with logic, numbers and words. They may not tell you anything you don't already know – but you might be surprised.

Personality tests, on the other hand, can give you real insight into your characteristics and preferences. They are particularly useful because they contain statements – often multiple choice – that act as prompts. So instead of asking yourself, 'How do I contribute to a team?', a personality test will give you a set of situations to choose from, which, taken together, will indicate how you usually behave. Personality tests and questionnaires are not magic – they only reflect back to you information you have put in, but in a systematic and logical way.

A well-known example readily accessible to students and graduates is Prospects Planner, on the Graduate Prospects website, which is designed to help career planning by producing a list of jobs that fit most closely with the answers you give in the questionnaire.

Employability skills

Skills that have particular currency in the job market are often referred to as employability skills. They are the skills and behaviours that enable you to interact and work with a range of different people, and they can be learned. Here is a reminder of the employability skills we listed and defined in Chapter 2 – look back if you need to remind yourself what some of these terms mean.

- self-management;
- resilience;
- teamwork;
- business and customer awareness;
- problem solving;
- project management;
- communication and literacy;
- numeracy;

- application of IT;

- foreign language skills.

It may not be obvious at first glance, but most degree courses provide opportunities to develop skills that transfer to the workplace. A connection between a degree in Theology and a career in the police might seem unlikely, but read what Andrew says.

 **example**

'My degree encouraged me to think beyond the expected norms, to challenge ideas and express that thinking. My work certainly demands that I look closely at any given situation and try to look beyond the glaringly obvious . . . whether working with a prisoner or developing new working practices. The close study and intricate dissection of theory, particularly in Theology, was responsible for developing these skills.'

Andrew, BA (Hons) Theology and Psychology, MTh postgraduate student

Find out more

Your university may offer sessions or online materials on how to develop your employability skills. Sometimes these sessions form part of your subject timetable; in other cases they are an optional extra. See what you can find out about what's on offer where you are. An Internet search for employability skills will also bring up useful questionnaires and checklists.

brilliant tip

In addition to the skills needed for a particular job, employers of graduates look for competence in a range of employability skills, so look for opportunities to learn about, develop and show evidence of these skills.

Making the connections

If you have followed this chapter through, you should now have a clearer idea about those aspects of yourself that help to determine your future choice. You might even have drawn up a summary of your own skills, interests and values. It may be important to add other information about yourself, for example your health and fitness, your family situation and your finances. In the final chapter of this handbook we will explore the impact of these other factors on your career plan. For now, let's think about how to make use of your new insights.

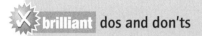 **brilliant** dos and don'ts

Do

✔ keep up to date with how your skills, interests and values change over time;

✔ seek out opportunities to develop your skills, through formal and informal learning;

✔ develop your interests with new experiences;

✔ examine job information for skills, interests and values as well as for the activities involved in the job.

Don't

✘ stand still – keep on learning, whatever the circumstances.

Try this exercise

Looking at your own skills, interests and values will help you to look at jobs in a new way. Think about your last part-time or vacation job – you might have taken it 'because it was there', or because you always work there in the vacation, or because your friend works there. For a few moments, think about this job and answer the following questions:

- What skills did you need, or use?

- In doing the job, what did it help to be interested in?

- What values did the organisation hold, either in a mission statement or in everyday working practice?

Now answer these questions for a graduate job you might think about doing:

- What skills will you need?

- What will it help to be interested in?

- What values are likely to be important?

You can find information about skills and interests in the entry requirements or person specification for the job. Information about values is harder to pin down. Though a company website will often quote the organisation's values, you need to think about the detail of a particular job to work out what the associated values might be.

 **recap**

- Knowing more about yourself, especially your skills, interests and values, will help with your career planning and jobsearch.

- Use the skill of reflection to develop your self-awareness and build your evidence.

- Employability skills are important in all jobs – work on yours.

- Get an in-depth insight into job opportunities by using the 'skills, interests and values' headings.

What to do next

- Use the ideas in this chapter to identify your skills, interests and values.

- Complete a 'Prospects Planner' to help with your career planning.

Work experience: making it purposeful

Work experience offers enormous benefits to you in your career planning and job seeking. It sometimes has a poor image – it's associated with school, it's boring, or it's exploitation. We will show you in this chapter that it need be none of these. You can choose and manage your work experience to suit your needs, and make it work for you.

Firstly, we need to be clear what we mean by work experience, and how it differs from work and employment.

 **brilliant** definition

Work – a purposeful activity that could be done as a paid job.

Examples from your everyday life include fixing a computer, delivering or collecting something for a friend, decorating a room, braiding someone's hair, giving some sports coaching. Reasons you might do this: to save money, because you enjoy it, are good at it, because friends will return the favour with something they can do, because you want to get more practice. Employment is simply work you get paid to do. So how does work experience fit in?

brilliant definition

Work experience – work that you do in order to develop your skills and knowledge. It is usually unpaid but, in some circumstances, such as sandwich placements and some internships, work experience is paid.

In the rest of this chapter, we will look at different kinds of work experience, how to access them and how you can benefit from them, and we'll show you how to get the best out of your work experience.

Five kinds of work experience

What you choose to do will depend on a number of factors, including how much time you have, what you want to achieve, and whether you really need to get work experience as an entry requirement for a graduate job or course. Later in the chapter we will look at the overall benefits of work experience, but first we need to be clear about the different kinds of opportunities covered in our definition. There are five main categories, each with its own particular benefit, or impact. We will illustrate some of these with real-life stories from graduates.

Volunteering

Volunteering is, by definition, something you offer to do without being paid. You might think it's about working for a charity, or fundraising for a good cause, but it also includes spending a couple of weeks in a law firm or a primary school in order to learn more about what goes on while making yourself useful. It could be one day a week, a block of time, or just a one-day event like beach cleaning or marshalling for a charity bike ride. A particular benefit is that employers see you as motivated because you are choosing to use your spare time constructively.

brilliant example

'In my second year I had to choose between studying abroad or having a work placement. I went abroad but realised at the start of my third year that I had missed out. I joined the local tourist board as a volunteer for two days a week, and learned many valuable skills which helped me to apply my studies to real-life situations. Towards the end of my third year a full-time job in the tourist board came up – I got it!'

Caroline, BA (Hons) Marketing and Tourism

How to get in

Some organisations are highly dependent on volunteers and may recruit on your campus with posters and display stands, but other opportunities are less visible. Follow our suggestions to find a really good volunteering opportunity.

✖ brilliant dos and don'ts

Do

✔ find the student volunteering organisers in your university. They help to 'match' volunteers to opportunities – you tell them what you would like to do and how much time you have, and they will make you an offer. You may need a CRB (Criminal Records Bureau) check, which they will help you with. Be aware that having a criminal record may not rule you out entirely but it may restrict the opportunities open to you;

✔ contact the volunteer bureau in your nearest town or city if you have already graduated – they will do the same job of matching you to what's available;

✔ make a direct approach by letter or email if you have an organisation in mind that isn't on the university's list of opportunities. This works especially when you want to spend a short block of time observing and learning – but make sure that you offer to do some work too. You need not be specific, just show willing! Help them by saying why you want to spend time there and what you hope to gain;

✔ ask people you know. We discuss networking in Chapter 1 'Accessing job opportunities'. Friends and relatives are useful as a way in, but remember firstly, that you will be in a work role in the organisation, not as a niece, godson or next-door neighbour; and secondly, that they may have stuck their neck out to get you in – so don't let them down.

Work placement as part of your course

Some courses include a work-based or employability module that can either be compulsory or optional. The extent to which you can choose what you do varies according to the university and the subject – but if you have the chance, it's well worth taking. Assessment may be based on the tasks you have carried out for the employer; or it may be about your own learning during the placement. This means what you have learned about yourself – your skills, interests and capabilities – as well as what you have learned about the organisation. The personal insights you get from this process of reflection will help with your career planning, and the particular benefit of a work placement is that it might lead to a job.

brilliant example

'As part of my Animal Behaviour and Welfare course I did a six-week placement with a charity that trains dogs to assist people with disabilities so that they are able to live more independently. The placement gave me the skills and experience to improve my chances with future job applications, as well as reconfirming that this was the area I wanted to pursue. A year later, the charity contacted me to offer me a temporary post for maternity cover. Four months after that I was offered a permanent post as the charity was expanding.'

Anna, BSc Animal Behaviour and Welfare

How to get in

Some universities have a department or team whose job it is to find placements for all students. This works well because relationships are built up between the university and employers over time and approaches are centrally coordinated. If this is the case at your university, make sure that you provide all the information you are asked for, within the deadlines set. This way you are more likely to get the kind of placement you want.

Other universities expect you to find your own placement. This offers you greater flexibility to tailor the placement more closely to your preferences, but it does also mean that you'll need to be proactive. Here's what to do.

brilliant dos and don'ts

Do

- think about the kind of experience you want, based on your career plans, your interests, and the gaps you would like to fill. Do think about talking this over with a tutor or a careers adviser;

- identify the organisations that are likely to fit the bill – ask your careers service, your tutors and your contacts. For possible leads, get inspiration from job advertisements and business directories, both in print and online;

- write a good letter of application, setting out what you want and why, e.g. 'a four-week work placement to apply the learning from my course in a commercial setting', (don't say 'because I have to do this for my course') and what you can offer while you are there. Check for spelling and punctuation and include your contact details. If you don't hear within say a fortnight, follow up with a polite phone call;

- start looking in plenty of time – six months ahead, more for a one-year placement.

Don't

settle for an easy option – your old school, your Saturday job, your uncle's firm – unless it really fits in with your career plan and adds value to your CV.

Work shadowing

This is usually a short spell, from one day up to a week, where you find out more about a job by accompanying someone who does that job in their daily work. The great thing is that you could spend time with anyone in an organisation, from a new graduate trainee to the chief executive. You're not expected to do their job, so you can really concentrate on observing, listening and learning about what they do, to build up your knowledge of a particular kind of work. It's low cost and relatively low effort for organisations, so it can be easier to set up than a longer placement or voluntary opportunity. The gain to you is that it opens up contacts and adds to your networking.

How to get in

Some universities offer work shadowing placements so check this out first. Otherwise, just look back at the dos and don'ts for getting your own work placement. The same principles apply, but this time you will be asking for the chance to shadow for a day, or a week, as a way to enhance your experience and knowledge. Also, remember that, for some roles in the public eye, you can observe informally, as Thomas's story illustrates.

▶ brilliant example

'So that I could see what a career as a barrister is like, I contacted various chambers to arrange mini-pupillages, the name given to a few days shadowing barristers in court and in meetings with clients. Not only did this give me an insight into a career at the Bar, but it meant I met barristers at various chambers. In my days off at university or in the holidays, I often went to court and sat in the public gallery observing cases, giving me more opportunity to see barristers in action and sometimes speaking to those I had spent time with on mini-pupillage.'

Thomas, LLB, LLM and Bar Professional Training course

The next two categories are a little different as they may involve payment, but are still work experience according to our definition.

Sandwich and vacation placements during your degree

These placements are either the whole of the penultimate year of your degree, or they fit into a vacation – usually, but not always, summer. They may not be assessed as part of your course. However, a course that is designed to include a sandwich year will require you to carry out the placement in order to pass your degree. Some vocational degrees like Engineering will expect you to undertake relevant vacation placements.

Travel and international trade and commerce have led to a rise in the number of courses with a 'year out', though some of these offer a year of study abroad rather than work experience. Here, we are using the term sandwich course to refer to four-year degree courses, which include a one-year placement in industry, typically in science, business or vocational programmes, such as quantity surveying or dietetics. There are particular benefits – a substantial, one-year placement can make a real difference to your job prospects because you have evidence to demonstrate what you can do. A vacation placement adds to your experience and demonstrates that you are purposeful in choosing how to spend your time off.

brilliant question and answer

Q What is the difference between a vacation placement and a vacation job?

A The difference is in the intention – the employer is offering you some work that will help you towards your degree, and may signal this with a clear 'vacation placement' label; and you are choosing to do it for the same reason.

How to get in

If your placement is a course requirement, there should be some help at the university, even if it's just the contact details of last year's placements. Otherwise, use websites such as Graduate Prospects and work experience directories from your careers service, and try personal contacts. Your part-time job in retail just might have something in management or buying if that's your interest.

Be prepared – more is expected of you at the application stage than for the shorter work placements in term-time, which we looked at earlier in the chapter. You may have to go through a full selection process, including application form and interview, so look at Chapters 10 and 11 'Making applications: getting past the first post' and 'Succeeding in selection' for pointers.

Internship after graduation

An internship is a relatively new term that refers to a period of planned work experience for graduates. It was introduced partly to offer something useful to graduates feeling the effects of the recession on their jobsearch; in an economic downturn there is usually an impact on the recruitment of new staff. Internships benefit employers too – organisations will need experienced and motivated applicants when the economy improves.

Some internships are paid, others are not. Whether you're entitled to payment will depend on what you actually do for the organisation – not what your role is called. If you are performing as a worker, you must be paid at least the national minimum wage. If you are taken on as a volunteer, you're unlikely to receive payment. Even if your internship is unpaid, however, it's worth asking whether the organisation could cover your expenses, such as daily travel costs.

The particular benefit is that some employers use an internship as an extension of the selection process, so you can demonstrate your suitability for the job in the workplace.

How to get in

Internships are advertised on websites such as Graduate Prospects and Graduate Talent Pool.

> ▶ **brilliant** example

'I came to realise that the people who get the graduate jobs are the people who had gained work experience during their time at university . . . I decided to take out a loan to support a political internship . . . Ultimately, it's all well and good having knowledge of a subject, but a practical ability to perform in a working environment is completely different. My eight-month internship involved working for three days a week in every imaginable part of political campaigning. What an eye opener! . . . after the election, I wrote to a dozen or so newly elected MPs explaining what I had been doing. Three days later I had an interview and was offered a job as a parliamentary assistant.'

Kevin, BSc (Hons) Politics

How you can benefit

Whichever kind of work experience you choose there are great gains to be had – and not only because you will be more attractive to an employer, though clearly this is important.

Personal confidence and transferable skills

Just being engaged in a purposeful activity that has clear outputs and helps other people out, either directly or indirectly, can give you a sense of achievement and a confidence boost. If you pick up some skills for employment, even better. The student in the following example volunteered within her university in a variety of roles, not obviously connected to her graduate job as an innovations researcher. Notice all the gains she made.

▶ brilliant example

'One of the voluntary roles I took on was as a student ambassador. I introduced new and potential students to the campus and showed them what was available to them on campus and the services open to them. Having been a new student previously myself, I knew how they felt and the need to help them settle in as soon as possible.

I also worked as a volunteer one day a week in a university department. This gave me a chance to experience an office environment and to see the university services from the other side of the counter. I undertook lots of different tasks, including general admin tasks and statistical analysis as well as helping out at different events put on by the department. It was a very team-oriented department, which taught me so much about the need to work as a team.'

Jo, BSc (Hons) Mathematics

In this one example, you will have noticed how Jo developed her experience of:

- communication skills;

- administration;

- statistical analysis;

- event management;

- working in a team.

Sometimes you just have to look beyond the surface to find the opportunities for learning. Think about working as a volunteer in a charity shop – a popular choice for people who want to help others. Firstly, there are job-related skills to learn, such as sorting stock, pricing up articles for sale, display, handling money and customer service. Then there are the transferable or 'soft' skills of working in a team, acting responsibly by turning up when you say you will, and interacting with all kinds of people. So what starts out as doing a good deed also becomes a great chance to learn.

Improving your job prospects

You might have noticed Kevin, in one of our case studies, saying that the people he knew who got graduate jobs were the ones who got work experience at university. It might sound obvious, but why does it work so well?

It works because it enables you to do all of the following.

Try things out

Firstly, you can try things out so that, by the time you are applying for a graduate job, you are much clearer about what you want and why, and you can say so in your application form and interview. Deciding that you don't want to pursue something is just as valuable as confirming that you do, and you might discover a kind of work, or an interest, that you didn't even know about.

Get experience

This isn't as obvious as it sounds. For some professional training courses it's essential to have relevant work experience before you can be considered. Examples are teaching, clinical psychology, physiotherapy; and for jobs and courses where it's not a requirement, it certainly helps to demonstrate your commitment and knowledge.

Collect and record evidence for your applications

We talk about the need for evidence in Chapter 10 'Making applications: getting past the first post', and work experience is one of your best opportunities. It's hard remembering in your final year the detail of that great work placement you did in your second year, so keep some kind of record of what you did, what you learned and what you achieved for each piece of work experience you have. It will make a real difference to your CV. Kevin, our brilliant example for internships, was able to replace his long list of part-time bar and retail jobs with a section headed 'Political work experience' and a much shorter 'Summary of other work experience'. His CV became targeted and relevant for the kind of job he wanted.

Enhance your jobsearch

Every work experience opportunity you take will give you some contacts, who may be helpful when you are looking for work. Even if they don't have a job to offer, they might know someone who does, or be willing to look at your CV.

Depending on how long you've been there and what you have done, work experience employers might be great for writing a reference for you. This is useful as most application forms ask for an academic and an employer reference. Remember to ask them first.

Give yourself structure and focus

This is particularly useful when you have graduated and you are still looking for your graduate job. Even if you are working, using days off or holidays to pursue your career goal with relevant work experience helps to remind you that your goal is still there. Thomas was our brilliant example for work shadowing, and this is how he is using work experience to keep in touch with his career aim of becoming a barrister.

brilliant example

'Since qualifying I have continued to apply for pupillage. In order to enhance my chances I have continued to complete a number of mini-pupillages at different chambers to broaden my experience and also make myself known to chambers before applying to them.

In order to gain more practical experience, I became a volunteer at an advice bureau. I conduct one-to-one interviews with clients weekly on a variety of different subjects. This has given me experience of dealing with different types of people as well as exploring a client's problem through questioning before advising them on the different options available.'

Thomas, LLB, LLM and Bar Professional Training course

How to make it work

If you have worked through this chapter you will now know about the different kinds of work experience, how to access them, and why work experience can be a real benefit in your career planning and jobsearch.

In this final section we tell you what to do, and what to avoid, to get the best from your work experience.

brilliant dos and don'ts

Do

- ✔ take control – be clear what you want and what you can offer and negotiate with the employer so that you both gain;
- ✔ reflect and review – think carefully about what you are learning and record it somewhere, so that you can refer to your experience in job applications;
- ✔ be aware that there are limits on hosting work experience in some job sectors, due to factors such as confidentiality and child protection – it may be easier if you use your university volunteering scheme or local volunteer bureau to set up your placement in sectors involving children, vulnerable adults, health services or offenders;

✔ notice and absorb the discipline and protocols of the workplace – what to wear, how people are addressed, how the phone is answered.

Don't

✘ give up – if you think that you are not getting any benefit, talk to the person in charge of your programme to see if some adjustments can be made. If it's a placement that forms part of your course, get the advice of your tutor;

✘ assume there's no value in a work experience opportunity without really thinking about it and giving it your best shot.

brilliant recap

- There are five different kinds of work experience, each with a particular benefit.

- There are also benefits that apply whichever kind you do.

- Work experience can help you to develop and learn about yourself as a person, and it can help with getting a brilliant graduate job.

- You can make it work for you – take control, be clear about what you want and what you can offer.

What to do next

- Think about how work experience could help you with your career plan.

- Consider what you want to (a) learn and (b) achieve?

- Use our 'How to get in' tips to get the work experience you want.

CHAPTER 9

Dates and deadlines: your timeline for action

Whether you enjoy planning, list making and target setting or whether you much prefer the adrenalin rush of a tight deadline or just letting fate take a hand, this chapter will help you to deal with the imposed deadlines and timescales involved in job seeking, and show you how to fit them into the other demands of your final year. We will tell you how to find out about critical deadlines, and how to manage application forms and interviews alongside academic assignments. It's never too soon to start – and, as you are reading this book, you are already under way.

Your time is your best resource

Your own time is one of your best resources; managing it well will not only help you achieve your graduate career, you will also develop a valuable skill for reducing stress at work and enriching your life outside work.

Managing your time is *not*:

- pre-planning every waking moment with lists and charts;
- losing out on spontaneous invitations;
- giving up the right to change your mind.

Managing your time as a student is about:

- having a sense of how much time you *need* to spend on: academic work; paid work; socialising; exercise and relaxing; and how much you *actually* spend – then making adjustments as needed to keep a good balance;

- knowing what your current projects are and when each deadline occurs;
- planning ahead to maximise performance and reduce pressure and unnecessary stress, as Kevin did in this brilliant example.

brilliant example

'First year was standard – just enough reading and scraping by on a couple of modules. Second year, I kicked on slightly – I wanted to go into my final year with a prospect of a 2:I, and I had seen friends with a backlog of failed modules – I didn't want that to happen to me.

I put extra work into my final year – it paid off and I achieved a first.'

Kevin, BA (Hons) Politics

Four critical factors

There are four critical factors you need to consider in creating a timeline for action while you are at university. These are:

1 devising a graduate job plan;
2 making the best use of your time at university to increase your employability;
3 early deadlines;
4 in your final year particularly, balancing job applications and interviews with the pressures of study.

Now let's look at each of these in turn.

Graduate job plan

Large or difficult tasks are more easily tackled if they are broken down into smaller tasks, so let's see what we can do with this very large task of getting a graduate job.

1   Decide what kind of areas you want to go for. If possible, book a one-to-one interview with your university careers adviser if you want to talk it through. You can also make use of online resources before you meet up – check out what your own university offers or visit some of our recommended sites.

If you don't know where to start, other chapters in this book should help. Remember that Part 1 covers what's out there, so you might want to use it to remind yourself of what the options are.

2   Prepare your CV and keep it updated. Use Chapter 10 'Making applications: getting past the first post' to help you get started.

3   Tell the people who will write references for you about your plans and give them a copy of your updated CV.

4   Check dates and deadlines, look at job advertisements, visit careers fairs.

5   Make applications for: jobs; postgraduate courses; internships.

6   Prepare for interviews: read (and act on!) Chapter 11 'Succeeding in selection'.

7   Get feedback – from employers who have interviewed you, employers who did not invite you to interview; friends and tutors.

If you have a look at this plan, you will see that:

● steps 1 and 2 are SLOW – they need the biggest investment of time, so you need to get started on this early in your final year or even sooner, perhaps in your first or second year;

● step 3 is QUICK but important – you may need to provide updates from time to time; and

● steps 4 to 7 are MEANDERING – less of a straight line and more of a cycle that you will repeat a number of times, and that you should spend some time on each week.

But note that time doesn't always pass at the same speed, and that some tasks are quick to do while others are slower. Anything that involves other people takes time to organise – for example, try to avoid getting someone to check over an application the day before it's due in – they may not be free, and you won't have time to make changes. You can't control other people, but you can control what you do and when you do it – so take advantage of that. Try to set aside some time each week for your graduate job plan.

 **example**

'The university can help in so many areas. The careers and employability team helped me to develop my CV before I started applying for graduate jobs, and the volunteering team helped me to organise some relevant work experience.'

Nicola, BSc (Hons) Forensic Biology

Increasing your employability

University life is full of opportunities to increase your attractiveness to graduate employers, while at the same time testing out your own ideas about your future career. If you struggled to think of something to say in your UCAS personal statement, then act early to ensure that you have plenty to say to a graduate employer about how you have spent your time at university and what kind of difference that has made to you as an employee.

In Chapter 8 'Work experience: making it purposeful', we talk at length about work experience, both paid and unpaid. Remember that, for some careers, relevant work experience is an essential requirement, so don't leave it too late. Your university careers service or job shop will help, and remember to use online resources too. Other activities to think about are: membership of student societies, particularly if you hold an office such as treasurer, secretary or publicity officer; representing your peers on a staff–student liaison committee; being a student ambassador on open days. Look at the following table in the brilliant example for the employability skills you could develop, and tell an employer about, with three of these examples.

 **example**

Role	Skills for employability
Treasurer, film society	Using communication, initiative and persuasion to raise funds; using numeracy and integrity to manage a budget; contributing to committee meetings
Student rep., staff student liaison committee	Listening, questioning and summarising to obtain and represent views of others; understanding the protocol of, and contributing to, formal meetings; advocacy and negotiation skills
Open-day ambassador	Customer relationships; communication to a mixed group (students and parents); tact, diplomacy

If you are still a student, try to map out the opportunities you have between now and graduation for becoming more employable. Include vacation work, paid part-time work, voluntary opportunities, work placements and other student activities.

Think also about your life outside university, especially if you are a home-based student. You still have time to find and enjoy activities that will make a difference to you, the applicant. This is not just about employability, but about presenting yourself as a well-rounded person – and enjoying what that feels like.

brilliant tip

Map out the opportunities between now and graduation for increasing what you can offer to a prospective employer.

Early deadlines

Next, let's look at early deadlines for postgraduate study and graduate jobs. These take many students by surprise, especially those who, perhaps understandably, assume that the beginning of their final year is the time for action. If you habitually hand in assignments at the last minute, now is the time to break the habit if you want to maximise your chances of securing a job in a competitive labour market.

Some organisations have a cut-off date and candidates can apply up to that date. Others operate a first-come, first-served approach, which means that, once the places are filled with suitable applicants, no more will be considered. That means you can't predict when exactly the application process will close. Either way, if you know what you want to apply for, it makes sense to apply early. This will give the impression that you are motivated and organised.

Ones to watch

- **Teaching**: the Postgraduate Certificate in Education (PGCE) application process starts in mid-September. That means you should be working on your application before you enter your final year. Check on **www.gttr.ac.uk** to see how soon you can apply and to find out more about the application process.

  Though there is no closing date for PCGE Secondary, popular subjects like PE and Art fill up very quickly. This means you should apply as soon as the process begins, which is usually mid-September.

  For PGCE Primary the closing date is 1 December, but many courses start interviewing before this date and there is a lot of competition for places. So your application needs to be submitted sooner rather than later.

- **Law**: applications to training courses to become a barrister (Bar Professional Training course) or to become a solicitor (Legal Practice course) must be made during the autumn term of your final year and no later than 1 December. Applications for training contracts (prospective solicitors) must be made by 31 July before you start your final year. For the Bar, applications for scholarships via the Inns of Court close on the first Friday of November.

- **Postgraduate courses**: some, for example Clinical Psychology, have a closing date of 1 December. Many have no published closing date, but will close when full. Don't be lulled into a false sense of security. Places are limited and, once a programme leader is sure that they have got enough applicants to fill all the places they have, they may well stop admitting to the programme or may only run a waiting list. Also, admissions tutors may well be away from the university over the summer. So, although it may be tempting to leave these applications until you have got through your finals, it may not be wise. You can find more information on **www.prospects.ac.uk** – go to postgraduate study, and look on the websites of individual universities if you know the course you want to do.

- **Graduate training schemes**: some have closing dates in the autumn term, so you need to be quick off the mark and well prepared in order to complete your application. Get information from your careers service – they will usually have multiple copies of graduate jobs directories early in the autumn term, and they will also advise you about useful websites.

Keep checking your careers service website and notice boards for deadline reminders.

brilliant tip

Know your deadlines and apply in good time – you will appear motivated and organised to employers and you will avoid last-minute panics.

Balancing job applications with final-year study

This is our fourth critical factor in managing dates and deadlines. We're not going to pretend that this is easy – but it is possible – and, somehow, you are going to have to do this. When the graduate job market is tough, you have to start earlier and keep going to get your job.

Having a clear schedule of your academic deadlines and workload is the essential first step. The next step is to carry out this work steadily and in good time. This way you will have some spare capacity for the unexpected job application.

Next, have the groundwork done in advance. In the next chapter we will look in detail at making applications. A key point to note now is to have a good, up-to-date CV to hand. It's great to refer to when you need to give details of qualifications and previous employment, with dates.

Next, be organised. Where possible, keep a photocopy of your applications, as many of the questions will be similar. This also means that you can remind yourself of what you said if you are called to interview.

Finally, be honest. Your tutors want you to get a good job and, while they might also expect full attendance in your final year, they will be flexible about time for interviews, so let them know if you are called for interview; ask them to help you to catch up with anything you missed. You also need to keep them informed so that if they are asked for a reference they can respond immediately.

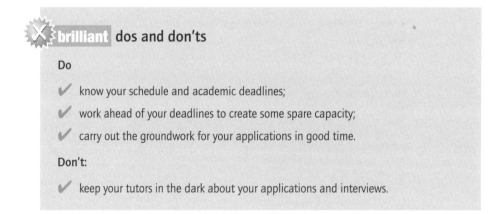

brilliant dos and don'ts

Do

✔ know your schedule and academic deadlines;

✔ work ahead of your deadlines to create some spare capacity;

✔ carry out the groundwork for your applications in good time.

Don't:

✔ keep your tutors in the dark about your applications and interviews.

Skills to help you

Managing dates and deadlines is a skill, or more accurately a set of skills. While it's true that some people might have a more natural aptitude, or preference, for planning ahead and juggling conflicting demands, it's also true that you can learn and you can improve with practice. Good time management, project planning and fact-finding skills are all invaluable in dealing with dates and deadlines. You may cover some or all of these in your academic curriculum, especially if your course includes study or learning skills or a work-related module. Good reference material abounds and some examples are listed in our 'useful reading'; here are some key points to give you a start or a reminder.

Project planning

 **definition**

A **project** is a piece of work that is carried out within a set timescale, with predetermined goals and agreed resources.

During your course you may have learned something about project planning and project management, especially if your course includes a work placement. This knowledge will be useful in the workplace, but it can also be applied to assignments, job hunting and even planning a holiday or a spell abroad. You can see how easily the examples just listed fit our brilliant definition. There are excellent resources to help you get to grips with project management, including software and reference books. Even something as simple as a countdown on your computer will keep you aware of the number of days left to a given deadline.

 **tip**

Treat job hunting like a project and it will become more concrete, manageable and achievable.

SMART project goals

Firstly, good project goals are SMART – **s**pecific, **m**easurable, **a**chievable, **r**ealistic and **t**imebound. Test out your current career goal – is it SMART? What do you need to do to smarten it up?

Look at this example of a graduate career goal, and think about how you would improve it:

Specific	A graduate training scheme
Measurable	Earning £25,000
Achievable	In a blue chip company
Realistic	Without moving from where I live now
Timebound	By Easter of my final year

Here are some of the questions we would ask about this career plan – compare them with your own thoughts.

Specific	A graduate training scheme	*In what industry or sector?*
Measurable	Earning £25,000	*How does this compare with what is on offer? Is this your bottom line or would you start lower if the prospects were good?*
Achievable	In a blue chip company	*Are you clear what you mean by this? Do you know what proportion of graduate jobs are offered in SMEs?*
Realistic	Without moving from where I live now	*What do you know about your local labour market? Can you achieve the other parts of this career goal without moving away?*
Timebound	By Easter of my final year	*Why this deadline? Does it fit with what you know about graduate recruitment?*

Milestones

Secondly, projects have milestones, or steps along the way that help you to break up the project into something more manageable and give you a sense of progress as you achieve each one. Go back to the graduate job plan earlier in this chapter and think about how you could create milestones from this plan.

Quality standards

Thirdly, projects have quality criteria to ensure that each piece of work that is produced towards the final project is of a good enough standard. You will need to 'quality assure' your CV, your applications and your interview technique. You can get objective and experienced feedback from your careers service; think about other people who might help, especially those in senior positions in employment who are used to recruiting staff.

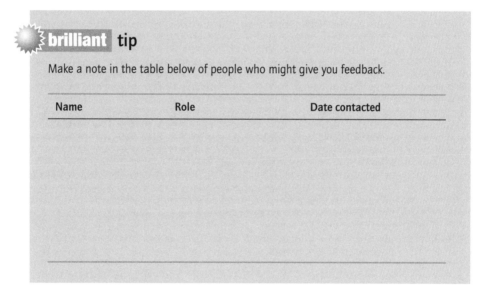

brilliant tip

Make a note in the table below of people who might give you feedback.

Name	Role	Date contacted

Managing your time

Earlier in this chapter we talked about time management: put simply, this involves balancing what you must do against what you enjoy doing. Even within work or study, some people spend more time than they need on aspects that interest them, at the expense of things they need to do but enjoy less.

How do you spend your time?

In the relative freedom of university life it's easy to get out of balance, reducing the time spent on academic work to the minimum, or prioritising your part-time job in order to keep your finances in control. So an honest assessment of how you actually spend your time each week, compared with what might be more reasonable, is a great start. As a guideline, full-time students are recommended to carry out no more than 16 hours' per week paid work, in order to keep enough time for academic work (and a social life).

Getting your friends to help

A really good tip to help you to manage your time is to have a friend or friends who will work with you, and to agree among yourselves a pattern of work nights, social nights, spells in the library and so on. The evenings you earmark for socialising might take advantage of special offers, such as two-for-one cinema tickets or a cheap deal for students in a local restaurant.

 **tip**

Make planning your time into a shared activity with one or two friends, so that you can keep each other organised.

Knowing what works for you

You should now be able to identify the periods of time each week that are for your academic work and your job search. These should be built around your own productive times of day – or night. Some university libraries are open 24 hours a day, recognising some students' preference for working late into the night when there may be fewer distractions – but be mindful of the 9 am lecture or early shift at work the next day.

The next step is getting the most out of these time slots, and there are two techniques that many people find really helpful.

Use a to do list

Using your schedule of academic deadlines and your graduate job plan, try starting each week with a list of jobs to be done. Then at the beginning of each day or study session decide what you will work on. Big tasks are daunting and difficult to start, so break them into smaller steps. For example, 'complete my application for Superstores Graduate Training Scheme' might have you staring at the screen or page, stalling at the more complex questions and putting it off until the day of the deadline. How might you break this task down into smaller steps?

You could:

- gather your factual information (qualifications, previous employment and so on, which should be to hand in your updated CV);

- research the company and the job information and identify aspects that you can include to indicate a good fit between you as an applicant and the company's values, aims and requirements;

- draft your personal statement/answers to open-ended questions and arrange for a careers adviser or tutor to have a look;

- set a day and time to clear away distractions and complete the form.

 **tip**

Break a large task into smaller achievable steps, each with a deadline.

Do the important/urgent test

The second useful tip is to use the important/urgent test. These two words don't mean the same! Urgent indicates a time deadline, while important refers to the impact of the task. So an assignment or a job application due in this week is both urgent and important, a decision early in your degree about your final-year dissertation topic is important but not urgent, signing up by 12 noon for a free coach for a night out is urgent but not important (you could get there on the bus, you could do something else), and deciding who'll do the food shopping next week is neither urgent nor important. The tasks on your career planning list should be in one of the following categories:

Urgent and important	Important but not urgent
Urgent but not important	Neither urgent nor important

It goes without saying that 'urgent and important' must be tackled first. In the workplace, 'urgent but not important' can often be dealt with by delegating; you probably don't have this option, but many tasks in this category are in any case relatively small and can be dealt with quickly and ticked off on your list.

'Not urgent and not important' tasks need to be kept under review in case they become urgent or important. In our earlier examples, next week's food shopping will become both urgent and important if the fridge and cupboards are empty; and your dissertation topic becomes urgent as well as important if it has to be formally approved in a week's time.

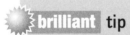 **tip**

Your own time is one of your best resources – and you are in charge of it.

Key dates: knowing where to look

Whatever your degree subject, you are almost certainly involved in researching information and developing good research skills. You need to apply these same skills to accessing good, up-to-date job information. Make sure that you know how this information is communicated at your university, for example through social networking sites, text messaging, email distribution lists, careers service websites and even posters and notice boards, and keep up to date. Your careers service may give you a list of graduate job websites and you may find others. Be aware that the Internet is unmoderated and don't assume that all websites are accurate and reliable.

Check that the website you are using is:

- **well presented** – written in grammatically correct English and free from spelling mistakes;

- **relevant to you** – e.g. suitable for higher education students seeking jobs in the UK;

- **up to date** – containing current information and with active external links;

- **authentic** – can you check the author? Is the website address genuine or passing itself off as something similar? Useful suffixes for websites are .gov for a local or national government body; .org for a non-profit making body or charity; .co.uk for a commercial company; .ac.uk for a UK educational body, and .edu for a US educational body.

 **tip**

Make sure that the graduate job websites you are using are accurate and reliable.

Tips for new graduates

If you have left university it doesn't mean that you have missed the boat for graduate jobs. Many employers have several recruitment points during the year, and many also recognise that there are some final-year students who choose to concentrate on getting a good result and defer their job search until after finals. However, compared with your situation when you were a student, there are some key differences that you need to tackle in order to manage your graduate plan.

- If you are working full-time you may find it more difficult to have time off for interviews, and consequently feel less motivated to keep on with your job search. Think about how best you can use days off, take unpaid leave or offer to work extra shifts to make up for lost time.

- Keep in touch with your university careers service. Are you on their email distribution list? Have you let them know that you are still working on your graduate plan and welcome their help? Are they running any workshops or bridging programmes to help you into work? If you have returned home after graduation, or moved to another part of the country, check out what your local university careers service might offer, for example information about local and regional opportunities. Don't forget to look online; check out the list of sites we recommend.

- Keep a record of the skills and experiences you are developing through the job you are currently doing. Graduates in direct-entry jobs often get early responsibility, so think about what being a bar supervisor or shop manager means for your future employability.

The rescue plan, for when things go wrong, the unexpected happens or you leave things to the last minute

In the context of your job search, things can and do go wrong. We've drawn up a list of nightmare scenarios – we haven't had to imagine these. They've happened to other graduate job seekers and that means they could happen to you. So what can go wrong?

- You miss a closing date.
- You are offered two job interviews on the same day.
- You're offered the job – but you have another job interview next week.
- There's a clash between a crucial piece of course work and the job interview of your dreams.
- You have two days to prepare a presentation for a job interview – and you are due to attend lectures.

Crises happen to the best organised of us – and in some of the situations above (two job interviews on the same day, for example) there's not much the individual jobseeker could have done to prevent it. It's how to proceed that's important. So here's what we would advise.

Honesty is the best policy

In these situations, honesty is pretty much always the best policy. Missing a closing date is of course to be avoided, but ask yourself what is the worst that can happen if you send your application form in late with a note of apology. The worst that can happen is that you will hear nothing more, but there is just a chance that there were no other suitable candidates, or that the firm will advertise again in due course and suggest that you reapply.

If you are offered two interviews on the same day, then you do need to decide which job you actually do prefer, now it has come down to it. Accept your preferred interview, then contact the other organisation (your second preference) and say that you already have an interview, so wonder if they can offer you another date. The worst that can happen is that they say no – but they might say yes.

The 'job offer with another interview next week' scenario is the one many students worry about, though it rarely happens. When it does, then do remember that you have been offered job number one, but the second job is by no means yours. What not to do is to ask employer number one if you can let him know next week after your second interview. This never goes down well and employer number one may well withdraw the offer and give the job to someone else. If the job on offer is what you want (and you shouldn't have got this far if it isn't) then accept it and withdraw from next week's interview. This is the only fair and honest thing to do.

The last two examples in our list of nightmare scenarios concern clashes between academic work and job hunting, so the obvious approach is to talk to your lecturer(s) for their advice. If there is no flexibility in your course work, then contact the employer and explain the circumstances; you may be offered another date. If not, then you must let this one go – the course work is both urgent and important.

The final example calls for some really firm time management on your part. How much time is at your disposal outside your lecture time? You may need to cancel other plans, but the chances are that you can draft out your presentation on day one, and get someone to look over it early on day two before you prepare the final version in the evening. This, after all, is what will happen at work, so it's good practice.

The golden rule, if you have a crisis or setback, is to stay positive and talk to a tutor or careers adviser.

 **recap**

- There are four critical factors in managing your time at university: having a graduate job plan; increasing your employability; anticipating early deadlines; and balancing job applications with final-year study.

- Important skills to develop are: project planning; time management; and knowing where to look for key dates.

- When things go wrong, stay calm, be honest and seek advice.

CHAPTER 10

Making applications: getting past the first post

Your written application to an employer is the all-important first impression. In this chapter we will take you through the different requirements of the application process and help you to make the best possible job of this first step. You might be the best interviewee in the world but without a good application you will never get to the interview stage.

Just to clarify, when we refer to applications we are including application forms, both paper and online, and also CVs and covering letters, which are the preferred application method of some employers. We will cover all of these, and share some tips for ensuring that you have made the best possible first impression. Special tips for applying for postgraduate study were covered in Chapter 6.

Which method of application?

A snapshot of 20 employers recruiting on the Graduate Prospects website indicated as many as eight different instructions for making the first approach. These ranged from asking applicants to contact the employer for more details (address and phone number given), through requests to send a CV by email or post, with or without a covering letter, to instructions to apply via the company website, usually entailing an online application form, but in two cases with the option to download, complete and send by post.

So the first message – and the first test – is to look carefully at what you are asked to do, and do it. If you attach your CV or a covering letter when it isn't asked for, you give the impression that you haven't read the instructions carefully enough or, even worse, that you think you know better than the employer. An error like this could mean that you are disregarded immediately.

 **tip**

Different employers have different requirements for the application process. Read instructions carefully and follow them exactly.

Getting started: information you need

Before you can start to prepare an application, you need the following information.

About yourself:

- **Qualifications**: what subjects, what grades, what year.
- **Employment**: dates of employment, job title, employer's name.
- **Voluntary and other spare-time activities**: dates, scope, location.
- **Skills and aptitudes**, with examples to provide evidence, drawn from your own experience.

About the job:

- Company information.
- Information specific to the job, usually a job description.
- Information on their ideal candidate, usually a person specification.

Preparing and updating your CV

 **definition**

A **CV** is a marketing tool that presents relevant facts about your life to date to prospective employers. CV is short for curriculum vitae, which means 'stream of life'.

Although not all employers ask for one, a full and up-to-date CV is a vital tool in your graduate job plan. It's a central place for information about yourself that you can cut and paste into an application form; it's great for speculative applications (when you don't know if a job exists but you want to show interest in an organisation) and for taking multiple copies with you to careers fairs.

☀ brilliant tip

You should always target your CV to the job or job area you are aiming for, so you may need to make some amendments to your CV each time you use it. Save each copy with a separate file name to remind you.

There are many good books and online guides that will help you to write your CV; in this series, for instance, have a look at *Brilliant CV* by Jim Bright and Joanne Earl, which contains some good guidance and useful examples of layout.

The big challenge for you as a graduate is to present yourself as a well-rounded individual with experience and interests outside your academic course, and with evidence of skills for employability and, where appropriate, business awareness. So we are going to give you some key guidelines here for strong graduate CVs.

Presentation

No more than two sides of A4; clear typeface such as Arial or Verdana at minimum font size of 11 pt; good layout with white space, consistent use of heading style using larger, bold or italic type rather than underlining; good quality, plain white paper for hard copies.

Structure

Most important information first, most recent first in each section. Although you might find CV templates on your computer, they can be limiting and it's better to have a go at your own layout. Start with your name, address, phone number(s) and email – no need for a 'Curriculum Vitae' heading as it will be obvious that it is a CV.

Important: is your email address suitable for use by an employer? Recent howlers in otherwise presentable CVs include: no1fashiondiva; igiveblondesabadname; pokeybabe; ibsexysam; and ratonthemat. Fine to use these for your personal emails, but not for job seeking. So either change your email or set up a new email account for job seeking (or use your university email address). Think about your voicemail too – don't be the graduate who almost lost a job in PR when the employer phoned her with the job offer to hear the voicemail message, 'Hi Babes, it's Juicy Lucy'.

brilliant tip

Make sure that your email address and voicemail message are professional and suitable for employers to use to contact you.

Content

Your key headings in order are: Personal profile
Qualifications
Employment
Skills and achievements
Referees

However, if you are a mature student with previous work experience you might prefer to start with skills and achievements rather than with qualifications. Getting the content of your CV right can be tricky, so let's look at these headings in more detail.

Personal profile

This is a good way of telling a busy employer the key facts about you and is particularly useful for new entrants to the labour market. A survey of employers conducted by Bright and Earl and described in *Brilliant CV* suggests that this kind of statement has a positive influence on recruiters. The act of writing it also helps to focus and summarise your goals. A couple of examples:

> A mature student of Forensic Science with previous experience in laboratory work, now seeking a first post that will enable me to apply my academic knowledge in the workplace.

> A second-year Business Studies student aiming for a graduate career in financial management and seeking a finance-based work placement in which I can begin to build my experience while making an active contribution to the organisation.

Qualifications

The key information is *what, when* and *where*.

It's important to include your current degree course – the dates will make clear that you have not yet obtained the qualification. Relevant modules, final-year dissertation topic and work placements are all important in a graduate CV, so work at presenting this information concisely.

Working backwards in time, A level subjects are important and so are grades if they are good. You may need to state grades anyway in an application form, but remember that your CV is your marketing tool so keep it positive and don't include failed subjects. *Never* lie – it just isn't worth it and if you are subsequently caught out you could lose your job.

For GCSEs, you don't need to list each subject but it's useful to indicate if you have English and Maths, so you might state:

> 2005 Anytown High School   GCSE: 10 passes including English and Maths;
>
> 5 Grade A, 4 Grade B, 1 Grade C

Include all academic qualifications here. Anything else – IT, first aid, sport qualifications – can usefully go in your 'skills and achievements' section.

Don't ever lie on your CV – would you really want to be doing a job knowing that at any minute someone could suss you out?

Carl Gilleard, Chief Executive, Association of Graduate Recruiters

Employment

Your next task is to outline your employment record, giving dates, name of employer, role undertaken and achievements in the role. List with present or most recent first, and be sure to include work placements and work experience, as these may be particularly relevant. Don't dismiss part-time and holiday jobs as having no value on your CV. Over time, as your working life develops, these early jobs might be replaced by more relevant, graduate employment, but for now they might offer useful evidence of the skills you have developed. For example, your short outline of a job as a sales assistant might state:

> Contributed to company sales targets, operated electronic till and stock control system. I was the first part-timer to be promoted to acting manager for my shift, and I devised and implemented an effective staff rota system, which was adopted in other branches.

Skills and achievements

This is a much better heading than 'other information' or 'hobbies and interests', though it can include these, because it's positive and presents information in a way that an employer can grasp. It's helpful to group this section under four or five bullet points, each with a theme. Here's an example based on IT skills to get you started:

> Computer literate: proficient in Microsoft Office, Internet and email; obtained ECDL (European Computer Driving Licence) in (give date).

You can include both 'hard' topics – sport, languages, workplace qualifications like first aid, health and safety – and 'soft' skills – communication, teamwork, leadership. For example:

> Effective team player: demonstrated through group projects in my degree, representing my year on the staff–student liaison committee, and my part-time work in a busy student bar.

References, testimonials and referees

brilliant **definitions**

A **reference** is a confidential statement about you that is sent direct from your referee to the employer.

A **testimonial** is an open document given to you, usually at the end of a period of employment, which you can use to support job applications, but which will not be accepted instead of a reference.

You may already have testimonials from previous employers; these are open, written statements about you which are given to you for you to use as you wish. Many people keep them in a portfolio along with exam certificates and, while they have value in offering evidence about you, they are not references and will not be accepted as such.

Employers use references for two purposes: to verify information supplied by the candidate; or to obtain information about the candidate's performance to date. Practice varies on how references are used in the selection process; in some cases they are not read until all other parts of the selection process are complete. Most employers seek specific information, either with a tick-box form or a set of structured questions; occasionally the referee is asked to write an unstructured statement.

If you are applying for a graduate job, you should ideally have two referees: an academic referee who knows about your performance on your degree course; and someone who can speak about your performance as an employee. Whether or not you include referees' details on your CV, you will certainly be asked for them on an application form.

Many universities have clear protocols about who can write your academic reference, usually your personal tutor or your dissertation tutor. It isn't just a matter of asking the tutor whom you like the best. So find out who will write your reference and make sure that they know what they need to know about you, your ambitions and your interests, so that they can support your application. Academic referees are particularly helpful if you have had any difficulties, such as illness, that have adversely affected your grades. In these circumstances they can offer evidence of your true potential.

For your employer reference, a work placement or voluntary work supervisor is a good choice especially if your placement relates to your chosen career. Alternatively, an employer for whom you have worked over an extended period will be able to comment on your skills in the workplace. At this stage in your life you should no longer need to ask sixth form tutors or your parents' friends, but should be able to call on people who have current or recent knowledge of you.

A final comment about referees. Once you have their permission (and you should always ask), you don't need to ask again each time you complete an application or send off your CV. But it is useful to keep your referees posted about your applications so that they can respond to requests quickly, or make arrangements to do so if they are going to be away at a critical period.

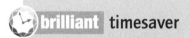 **timesaver**

Keep your referees up to date with your jobsearch progress, so that they can be sure to to respond quickly when asked for a reference.

If you follow our guidelines you should be able to produce a good, standard CV that you can take with you to careers fairs, and that you can adapt for particular jobs as needed, by rewriting your personal profile or by emphasising particular skills and achievements.

Before you use your CV, get it checked by a careers adviser or friendly employer and take notice of their feedback. Remember to keep your CV up to date, and to target it to the job you are aiming for.

brilliant recap

- Remember that your CV is a marketing tool.

- Pay attention to presentation, structure and content.

- Have it checked by an expert.

- Choose and brief your referees so that they can give a full account of you.

- Keep your CV up to date.

- Target your CV to each job you apply for.

Gathering information about the company and the job

Application forms and covering letters are always targeted to a particular job so, before we can consider these, we need to look at how to gather together everything you can discover about the job, starting with the company itself. This will be vital background for your application, and companies will in any case look for evidence that you have done your homework.

The company

Think about the different ways you can find out about a company or public sector organisation. Then have a look at our ideas below:

- company website;

- newspaper articles on the business pages;

- friends, tutors, careers advisers;

- information in the application pack you may have been sent;

- for schools, Ofsted reports and prospectuses;

- visit if there is public access, e.g. a retail company, a gallery or museum.

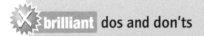

brilliant dos and don'ts

Do

✔ prepare in good time – at the application stage, not the day before the interview;

✔ ask yourself some questions that may come up at interview or even in the application stage. What is the 'company image'? Who are the key competitors? What are their successes? What is distinctive about them? Why are you attracted to working for them?

Don't

✘ rely on what someone else has said – find out for yourself;

✘ leave this research till the last minute.

The job

Once you feel confident that you know something about the company, turn your attention to the job itself.

There are two key pieces of information about any job:

- the job description, which lists the tasks the post holder will undertake; and

- the person specification, which lists the characteristics the employer wants the postholder to have, or criteria they must meet.

In some organisations these will be written statements made available to you before you complete your application; in others, all you might have to go on will be the wording in the job advertisement. While the job description is important and you will need to feel confident about it and interested in what it tells you, the person specification is essential if you are to make a good job of your application.

The person specification

Usually, criteria are divided into areas such as qualifications, experience, skills and aptitudes, and personal qualities, and each criterion is categorised as *essential* or *desirable*.

◆ brilliant definitions

Essential criteria are those that candidates *must* meet in order to be considered for interview.

Desirable criteria are optional extras that employers would like candidates to have, but are not a requirement of the job.

For example, while it may be essential to have a degree, it may be desirable to have a degree in specific subjects. While competence in Microsoft Office might be essential, ability to use specialist software may be desirable. Relevant employment experience may be either essential or desirable. Usually, desirable criteria are those that the candidate could achieve once in the job.

As a general rule, the words essential and desirable in this context mean just what they say and it is good, fair recruitment practice to apply them rigorously, so it would not be worth applying for a job if you do not meet the essential requirements. If, however, you are close, you might take a chance with an appropriately worded covering letter, for example:

> Although I note that you require two years' experience, I have successfully completed eighteen months in my current post which is a two-year contract and I would be very glad if you would consider me.

Desirable criteria are just that – the ideal candidate would meet these in addition to the essential criteria. So can you indicate that you could meet these criteria in due course? For example:

> My German is not yet fluent but I can hold a basic conversation and would be keen to carry out intensive training to increase my proficiency with technical and business language.

It's really important that you demonstrate in your application that you have read the person specification and that you offer evidence to show how you meet the criteria.

 **tip**

Show in your application that you fit the criteria set by the employer and that you are willing to work towards the desirable criteria where possible.

Application forms

An application form is a proforma used by an organisation as the first stage of the selection process. Information required on application forms falls into two categories: factual, for which your CV will provide an excellent quick reference; and job-related, which may take the form of open questions or an unstructured personal statement.

Some organisations have a general application form and therefore some parts might be difficult to complete in certain circumstances, for example, if you are still in your final year as a student and are asked for details of your current employment. Usually common sense will guide you, but do ask for help from your careers service or from a tutor if you are not sure.

Three formats

Employers may offer their application forms in one of three formats:

- **paper** – you will need to ask for a form to be sent to you, and you post it after completion. You will need to hand write most of the form, but may be able to attach a typed personal statement;

- **downloadable from a website** – to be completed and posted or emailed. You will be able to type into your downloaded and saved copy of the form;

- **online** – you locate the form on a website, complete and submit it electronically.

Completing your form

We'll talk about the content of your form shortly but first, here are some pointers to help you.

Whether your form is paper, downloadable or online, you need to set time and space aside to complete it, preferably well ahead of the deadline so that you have time to revisit what you have written and get someone to look over it for accuracy and clarity. Where possible make a draft copy and only when you are happy with it complete the final version. Take great care with presentation – forms do need to be free from spelling mistakes and crossings-out. If you are posting a paper copy, keep it clean and free from stains, marks and creases.

While each application *must* be tailored to the job for which you are applying, there will be some repetition, so it's good practice to keep a paper or electronic file of completed applications so that you can remind yourself of how you answered a similar question on a previous occasion.

brilliant tips

- Set time and space aside to complete your form, well ahead of the deadline.
- Where possible, make a draft copy of your form and complete this first.
- Aim for excellent presentation and accuracy.
- Keep a copy for future reference.

Online applications

While online applications are becoming more common, the principles of completion are the same as for the other two formats. However, there are some key differences with online forms. In particular:

- the word limit for more open questions might be rigidly applied;
- the opportunity for someone else to check what you have written may be more limited (though sometimes you can download the form to prepare a draft);
- you may be automatically deselected for something that you believe not to be relevant, e.g. insufficient UCAS points;
- you may not easily be able to keep a copy for reference.

There are ways around some of the obstacles that people put in your way. There are lots of employers who are not looking for the 2:1, so seek them out.

Carl Gilleard, Chief Executive, Association of Graduate Recruiters

Factual information

Your CV will provide an excellent quick reference for the factual information sought on application forms, which is usually about education, qualifications and employment experience, but read the instructions carefully. You may, for instance, be asked for information in chronological order rather than most recent first. Also, you may be asked to list all the examinations you have taken, whether passed or failed. This part of a form can be tedious to do but, once you have done it for the first time, you have it to hand for the future.

Open questions

We mentioned at the beginning of this section on application forms that job-related information is obtained in two ways: open questions and personal statements. We'll start with open questions.

Here is a set of questions based on a real application form. For each question there is a limit of 300 words.

> What are your skills, experiences and personality characteristics that make you suitable for a job in this organisation?
>
> Why do you want to work in the retail sector and in this organisation?
>
> Which of this organisation's current initiatives/projects most interest you and why?

Have a look at these questions and note down:

1   what you think the employer is looking for;

2   what you think you need in order to answer the questions.

Although this may look like a daunting task, it should help you to see that the groundwork done for this application could well help you with others.

Now have a look at our ideas.

Question	What employer is looking for	What you need
What are your skills, experiences and personality characteristics that make you suitable for a job in this organisation?	Your awareness of the person specification for the job and the extent to which you can demonstrate that you are a good fit.	Good, honest self-awareness. A range of evidence to support your statements about yourself. Job and company knowledge.
Why do you want to work in the retail sector and in this organisation?	Your motivation – why retail, why this company? An answer that shows your understanding of the sector and of the distinctiveness of the organisation.	Good knowledge and understanding of the sector and some clear reasons for your choice. Knowledge of the company and how it differs from its key competitors.
Which of this organisation's current initiatives / projects most interest you and why?	Your ability to research and to critically analyse. An indication of your own preferred career direction.	Time to do your homework. An understanding of the techniques of critical analysis. A sense of how your career might develop with this organisation.

Here is another, quite common, example of a set of questions for an application form. This time the format is different: you are asked to use evidence from your previous experience to demonstrate the skills in question.

In each of the following five boxes tell us about an incident that demonstrates your use of the skill named at the beginning of the box. You have 250 words for each box.

Communication

Teamwork

Problem solving

▶

Overcoming a setback

Ability to work under pressure

To answer these questions well it helps to follow a structure. The one we recommend is STAR, which stands for

Situation

Task

Action

Result

So you outline the **s**ituation, describe the **t**ask, say what **a**ction you took, and state the **r**esult. Here is an example of overcoming a setback, using the STAR framework. We have put the headings in to help you, but you would not include them on your application form.

▶ brilliant example

(*Situation*) In my second year I successfully applied to complete a work placement in a small but expanding marketing company. I was delighted to secure such a competitive placement. With just two weeks to go, the placement was cancelled due to illness.

(*Task*) I needed to find another placement, or I would have to wait until the summer vacation, which would mean deferring my assessment. The work placement office could offer me an alternative but not in marketing, which is my career aim.

(*Action*) So I thought about departments in the university that might benefit from a marketing project. I approached the careers service because I knew that students who used the service found it really good, but that there were many students who didn't know about it. I offered to design and carry out a survey of student perceptions and to make some proposals about marketing and publicity arising from the findings of the survey. I worked closely with careers service staff and got some advice from my tutor about designing the survey and analysing the results.

(*Result*) I presented the findings to the careers team and in the last two weeks of my placement began to work on a promotional campaign for the new academic year. I was offered the opportunity to continue to work in the careers service on a voluntary basis during my final year, so I have assisted in the implementation of the campaign and regularly speak to groups of students to promote the careers service. After the initial disappointment at losing my placement, my action in securing an alternative has meant that I have seen my project through to implementation and had the chance to do some really useful voluntary work. (*287 words*)

In the examples we have given there is a clear word limit. In online applications you will be cut off once the word limit has been reached, even if you are in mid-sentence, so it's essential that you draft your answers, check the word count and spelling, then cut and paste into the form. One of the workplace skills you need to develop is the ability to be concise, so the practice you get with your application forms will be put to good use in your working life.

 **brilliant** tip

Where you have open-ended questions with word limits, draft then cut and paste into your form.

Personal statements and covering letters

Similarities

Both personal statements and covering letters are opportunities to 'make your case' as an applicant. It should be clear from the employer's instructions which you are being asked to supply. Usually, a personal statement is a section of an application form, while a covering letter is sent to accompany a CV. Here are some dos and dont's that apply to both.

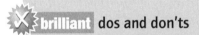 **dos and don'ts**

Do

✔ write in the first person;

✔ tell the employer why you are suitable for the job, and why you want to work for this particular employer;

✔ draw attention to your CV in the content of your covering letter, rather than simply attaching it. Say something like, 'You will see from my application form/CV that I have the qualifications required for this post.'

Don't

✘ begin every sentence with 'I';

✘ duplicate information you have already provided on your application form or CV.

Differences

So, although the purpose and content is much the same, how are personal statements and covering letters different from each other? It's mainly a matter of layout.

A personal statement is part of, or attached to, an application form, and written in prose with your name at the top of each sheet. There may be a word limit or more commonly a size limit – 'not more than two sides of A4' is a common example and also a useful guideline.

A covering letter is set out like a letter, with your address at the top right, the employer's name and address a little lower down on the left, followed by the date and any reference number you have been asked to quote.

Personal statements

Sometimes personal statements are unstructured, for example 'use this space to supply additional information in support of your application'. Or you may be given a structure – something like:

Use the space below and up to one additional sheet to tell us:

1 why you are suitable for this job and what you will bring to the organisation;

2 why you want to work for this organisation;

3 what your personal strengths and weaknesses are;

4 where you see yourself in 10 years' time.

Usually it helps to have a structure – but note that these questions, which are fairly typical, contain two traps for the unwary. For question 3, rather than listing your weaknesses, write instead about aspects that you would like to develop. For example, 'I have limited experience of writing bids for funding, but this is an area that I am keen to develop and look forward to gaining the necessary knowledge and skill.' The second trap is question 4, the 10 years' time question. A safe and acceptable answer is that you are keen to gain experience and then to identify areas of particular interest in which you might specialise – you may need to vary this according to the sector for which you are applying.

Covering letters

Though you may occasionally be asked for a covering letter with an application form, it is more commonly paired with a CV. You will see references in job adverts to 'apply by CV and covering letter'.

Try to find out the name of the person to whom you are applying, so that you can write Dear Mr Jones or Dear Ms Smith. Even if you are sending your covering letter by email it is good form to set it out like a letter, though you could omit your address and theirs from the top.

Although some people recommend a one-page covering letter, this can be difficult to achieve if you are demonstrating that you fit a fairly detailed person specification, so we would say a maximum of two pages – certainly no more. Where a 'letter of application' rather than a covering letter is asked for – common in teaching posts – this certainly means a two-page response, which clearly demonstrates how you meet the person specification.

Creating a structure

Whether it's a personal statement or a covering letter, your starting point is a rather frightening blank screen in front of you. So, just as with other pieces of writing, you need to think about introduction, middle and conclusion.

Introduction

Say what you are applying for in the first sentence. For example, for a covering letter:

> I write in response to your advertisement on the Graduate Prospects website for a trainee sales negotiatior in your Bristol office, reference number xxxxx.

To start a personal statement for the same job, you could say:

> I offer the following information in support of my application for the post of trainee sales negotiatior in your Bristol office.

Middle

Firstly, you need to make clear why you are suitable for the job, using the person specification or information from the job advert if no person specification is available. You need to offer evidence in support of your claims; here are some examples to help you.

> As a member of the university IT helpdesk, I have developed excellent communication skills, especially listening, questioning and clarifying, so that faults can be recorded accurately and responded to promptly.

> In my role as a shift leader in the student bar, I motivate and encourage bar staff to achieve high levels of customer service, especially when we are all working under pressure.

> I can work to high levels of accuracy in the laboratory following experience gained in my work placement and in research for my final-year dissertation.

Next, you need to say why you want this job, with this employer, without sounding cheesy. So you need to construct a sentence about your career plan, followed by a sentence or two about what attracts you to this employer. For example:

Having researched the career options open to an English graduate, I soon focused on publishing, a choice that became even more certain during a successful work placement during my last summer vacation. Your company has an excellent record of publishing first novels, an area of interest of mine and, having spoken to members of your team at a recent graduate fair, I know that you offer good training and prospects to graduate entrants. I would be excited to be part of your organisation.

Conclusion

Finish with a courteous ending that reinforces your motivation for applying for this post. Never write 'do not hesitate to contact me'. This is a negative ('do not') and over-used statement attempting to invite a positive action, and a waste of words. 'Please contact me' is much better. In the case of the covering letter, it's worth repeating your contact details.

Finish a covering letter like this:

Thank you for reading my letter. Please contact me at any time on 07654 321098, or by email at **jsmith@hotmail.co.uk**. I would welcome the opportunity of an interview and look forward to hearing from you.

Yours sincerely
(or Yours faithfully if you don't have a name and have written to 'Dear Sir or Madam')

(if posting a hard copy, sign legibly here).

Finish a personal statement like this:

I hope that this information has persuaded you to consider me for interview. I am very keen to be part of your organisation and look forward to hearing from you.

Speculative letters

Sometimes you may want to approach an employer without knowing if a job exists, but because you are attracted to the organisation. This strategy sometimes pays off, especially with smaller organisations. Advertising is costly and if your letter arrives just as someone hands in their notice, or just as expansion plans are being discussed, then you may get a response.

Your wording needs to be a little different from the covering letters we have already discussed, as you are not responding to an advertisement.

You need a strong opening paragraph that encourages the reader to carry on. You need to state:

- why you are writing to this company in particular;
- what role you are looking for;
- what you are offering.

For example:

> I am relocating to Anytown and note from your website that you are expanding your company. I am a graduate seeking a first post in technical sales and, as part of my degree, I successfully completed a year-long placement with a major medical equipment supplier.

In the body of the letter you can expand on your suitability and experience, but remember that you are attaching your CV so don't just duplicate its contents. Conclude as in our cover letter example above, with clearly stated contact details to make life easier for the employer.

 **tip**

Your signature on a covering letter should be clear and should include your first and last name. An illegible scrawl just looks arrogant.

Getting feedback and getting help

It can be hugely disheartening to send off dozens of applications and hear nothing back. Many job adverts state that only successful candidates will be contacted. Some say that if an applicant hasn't heard by a given date then they have not been shortlisted, but often it's a guessing game. While it's quite reasonable to contact the employer and ask if they have shortlisted yet, you would be very unlikely to get feedback on an application form alone, as this would be massively time consuming for most employers.

While it's possible that you have just been unlucky, if you have sent large numbers of applications for jobs for which you are suitable, and have not been invited for interview, then there may be a problem with your applications.

So get some expert help – go to a careers adviser, a tutor or someone you know who recruits graduates, and show them some of your recent applications. They may well spot a possible reason, most commonly that the applications are not sufficiently targeted to the employer and the job. Get the same person to look over your next application before you send it to check that you are not making the same mistakes again.

 **brilliant** tip

> If your applications don't lead to interviews, get someone to look at them and give you feedback.

Imagine you are the employer

Finally, put yourself in the employer's shoes. Imagine that you run a small enterprise and you have advertised a graduate post, inviting applicants to use downloadable application forms. Over 100 applications for a graduate trainee post in your growing company have arrived and are on your desk. You have to draw up a shortlist, and fast.

You have beside you the details of the job that the candidates received, which include a person specification you spent ages drawing up. This specification was clear about the kind of person and even subdivided the criteria into essential and desirable.

You will probably do a rough sort first, perhaps into three piles of yes, maybe and no. What would make you likely to put an application form into the 'no' pile? Think about this, perhaps make some notes, then look at the list below.

Common reasons for rejecting an application

- No evidence of meeting essential requirements (usually qualifications and/or experience).

- Scruffy form, e.g. creases, food marks, crossings out.

- Poor spelling and punctutation.

- Periods of time unaccounted for by education, work, travel, career break.

- No reference to the company/job.

- No attempt to demonstrate how/why the applicant is suitable for the job.

The more applicants there are, the more rigorously these sorting criteria will be applied, because the employer needs to arrive at a manageable number for interview.

The image of the employer with a huge pile of forms to sift through is one to hold on to as you are preparing and checking your application. In addition to matching the person specification, most employers are looking for the same things at this stage – good written communication, motivation, and that indefinable 'something extra'.

 **tip**

Visualise the employer reading your application. Will it go into the 'Yes' pile?

And finally, make sure that you check everything that you send to an employer. Use your spellchecker, your university careers service, your tutors and trusted friends.

To get an interview you need a good application. To get the job, you need a good interview, so have a look at Chapter 11 when you are ready.

What to do next

- Prepare your CV and have it checked.

- Think about who your referees might be and talk to them about your plans.

- Create a folder for application forms, personal statements and covering letters.

CHAPTER 11

Succeeding in selection

W e are now going on to the next stage of the selection process. If you have been called for interview, then you can assume that you have made a good start with your application form or CV. Hold this thought in your mind, and you will approach the next stage with confidence.

There are several good printed and online sources of help with all of the areas we are going to consider in this chapter and we will direct you to some of these but first, let's think about what employers are seeking to achieve.

The employer's perspective

Employers need to choose candidates who have the potential to be successful in the job – not an easy task, when applicants may not have had the opportunity to carry out similar work and may not, therefore, be in a position to offer evidence of success. While the interview is the most popular method of selection – and a strong predictor of success in the job – it is usual for other selection methods to be used alongside:

- In order to assess your *skills*, employers will usually break down the role into smaller components, for example managing a project, or working in a team, which they can find a way to assess.

- Employers may also want to find out if you have the specific *knowledge* needed for the job. They will make some assumptions based on your degree content, but may also test you through exercises, scenarios and case studies.

- An important question for employers is whether or not you will fit in, so they may look at aspects of your *behaviour* and *personality*, including your motivation – *why* do you want the job?

From your point of view (as the candidate), a range of selection methods is helpful because it gives you more chances to succeed and you can offset poor performance in one area by showing your strengths in another. For example, some people are not comfortable contributing to an unstructured group discussion, but can show excellent leadership in a group task.

 **brilliant** tip

Employers use the selection process to look for skills, knowledge and motivation.

Next, we'll look at tests, interviews and assessment centres in turn, outlining what to expect and giving some pointers for good preparation.

Tests

We talked about psychometric tests in Chapter 7 as aids to help you to know more about yourself. They are also used by employers to measure candidates' performance against either:

- the performance of an identified group in the population (graduates, adults, Year 11 pupils, a group in the same profession), known as norm referencing; or

- the standards or criteria determined by the employer, known as criterion referencing.

Psychometric tests must be objective, valid and reliable. In other words, they must be designed to: treat everyone who completes them in the same way so that scores can be compared; be relevant for the purpose and measure what they set out to measure; be consistent in the scores they produce, both over time and across similar groups of candidates. A quiz in a magazine, though interesting to do, is not objective, valid and reliable in comparison to a well-established personality test.

Kinds of tests

Most tests fall into one of two categories:

- **Ability/aptitude**: e.g. verbal, numerical and abstract reasoning tests, examine your ability to think logically and to problem solve, using words, numbers, diagrams, shapes or pictures. These tests consist of questions with right and wrong answers, and they should not depend too heavily on what you have learned at university, unless they are for a job-specific aptitude, e.g. in computing. Questions are often multiple choice, which should enable you to work more quickly. You will find lots of sample questions in books on how to succeed in psychometric tests – some titles are included in our useful reading list at the end of this book.

- **Personality**: e.g. leadership, teamwork, creativity measures are usually questionnaires; the questions often ask what you would prefer in a choice of situations, or how you would behave in a given set of circumstances. Employers may not see how you have answered individual questions, but will have a profile or summary that tells them about how you typically respond. While these tests don't usually have right and wrong answers (and shouldn't really be called tests), employers will often have a preference for what kind of person they are looking for. They may be looking for evidence of your ability to act decisively, or exploring your preference for working in a team or alone.

 **tip**

In a timed test, do as much as you can – don't waste time on a difficult question.

Most tests are time-limited, and are administered either online or in conditions that will remind you of taking an exam. An online test is often used as a first stage in selection, with successful candidates invited to the next stage.

Exam conditions are not meant to add stress, but are to ensure that candidates' results can be meaningfully compared with others, as all will have carried out the test in the same conditions.

How to prepare

brilliant dos and don'ts

Do

✔ practise – use 'how to' books and online practice sites, and ask your careers service if they run practice sessions;

✔ try to do it in 'test conditions' when you practise – no interruptions or distractions, working to a time limit;

✔ find out as much as you can about what to expect – look at the employers' information online or in print;

✔ read letters and emails carefully: check what the employer is looking for and get the basics right, such as when and where the tests will take place;

✔ be aware that some online tests are lengthy and you may not have much notice. Be prepared to rearrange your schedule to clear a time and space to work on it without interruptions or distractions.

Don't

✘ linger over a difficult question. Move on to the next – a good strategy in a timed test is to answer as many questions as you can;

✘ guess at random in a timed test as you may be penalised for wrong answers;

✘ leave it to the last minute: it won't help your performance;

✘ try to get out of it or offer excuses for lack of time.

Interviews

A job interview should not be a contest between two opponents – both you and the employer want the job to be filled. The vacancy is a problem to be solved, and both of you are on the same side of the problem. Employers want to get it right – it is costly to advertise, interview and appoint and they don't want to have to do it again – and you want to be a successful candidate.

▶ brilliant example

'I was a bit unsure as to how to approach finding jobs in the area of nutrition. I approached the university careers service and they gave me guidance, helped me prepare for interviews and informed me about the type of conditions to expect in an interview.'

Adam, MSc Public Nutrition

In the book *Brilliant Answers to Interview Questions* the author, Susan Hodgson, provides an excellent summary of the purpose of interviews. She says:

Interviewers are seeking the answers to three fundamental questions: Can you do the job? Will you do the job? Will you fit in?

Break the interview down

Like all challenging tasks, tackle this one by breaking it down into three stages:

- general preparation before the interview;
- during the interview;
- after the interview.

General preparation before the interview

- **Research the organisation and the job**. You will have done this already for your application form – do it again, go deeper this time, talk to people who work there or are in similar work. Who are their main competitors? Where does the revenue come from?

- **Check your invitation to interview**. This may sound obvious, but make sure you know where you are going, how you will get there and how long it takes. If you are driving, where will you park? Arriving in good time isn't just good manners, it will help you to feel calmer and more confident.

- **Decide what to wear and take**. No matter how informal the dress code is for the people who already work there, there is usually an expectation that interview candidates will dress fairly formally and conventionally. This doesn't mean an expensive suit that you will never wear again, but it does usually mean a smart suit or jacket and trousers, and a shirt and tie for males, and a smart suit or jacket and skirt/trousers with a shirt, blouse or top for women. If you are worried about your student budget, tour the charity shops for great bargains. Above all, make sure that your outfit – including footwear – is clean and well fitting, and that you can be comfortable without even thinking about what you are wearing. Check your personal grooming, and keep make-up, jewellery and perfume understated. Take with you as little as possible, in a neat bag or briefcase. If the interview requires you to take some documents (proof of identity, qualifications, sample lesson plans for a teaching post), put them in a tidy folder.

- **Just before the interview**. Your final preparation means checking that your phone is switched off, staying calm and quiet, being pleasant to other candidates if they are present, and to any staff you meet – but focusing on yourself with a few deep breaths until you are called in.

brilliant tip

Look and feel smart, ditch the clutter, and you will be able to focus totally on the interview.

Question preparation

Remember those three questions we looked at earlier – Can you do the job? Will you do the job? Will you fit in? – and think about how you will demonstrate that the answer is yes to all three. Employers increasingly want evidence to back up candidates' answers, so think of examples that will illustrate your ability to solve a problem, work in a team, manage your time under pressure, meet targets, follow instructions, lead others and so on. This might seem impossible – but think about not just your academic work but your part-time and vacation jobs, voluntary work and activities in student societies and sports teams.

What evidence can you offer to support the following skills? Make a note of your answers.

Skill	Evidence
Solving problems	
Working in a team	
Managing your time under pressure	
Meeting targets	
Following instructions	

The question 'Will you do the job?' is a tricky one and it's about motivation. So an employer will ask you why you have applied and how you see your career progressing. No one expects you to have had a lifelong ambition to work for a specific organisation, and employers will realise that you might have several applications under way at the same time. What they are looking for are signs of planning and of choosing their organisation because it offers the opportunity for you to do what you want to do.

There are some great examples of interview questions and answers in our companion publication *Brilliant Answers to Tough Interview Questions* – more details in the 'Further reading' section at the end of the book. While it would be a mistake to learn an answer by heart, the examples given will be a big help in your preparation.

Graduates need to ask where they fit into the critical path within the business process. What do I look for in an employee? The attributes that are important to any business: honesty, integrity, loyalty and reliability. Why reliability? It's pretty obvious: because we're a business. It winds us up terribly if somebody doesn't turn up and doesn't have have the decency to phone and explain. Or walks in late, not saying anything to the manager. Nothing winds us up more.

Julian Radley, Director, Evotel Holdings

During the interview

First impressions count!

A smile will help you to relax as well as giving a good impression. Experienced interviewers know that candidates are nervous and will do their best to settle you down. Wait to be invited to sit and shown which is your chair. If there is more than one interviewer (which is usual), make eye contact with them all – often those who did not ask the question are listening most intently to the answer.

Open and closed questions

Most interview questions will be 'open' – tell me about . . . describe a situation when you . . . how difficult did you find . . . If you get the occasional 'closed' question, such as 'Did you enjoy your degree course?', then give a full answer – they want more than yes or no.

 **tip**

Smile at the start of your interview, wait to be invited to sit, and make eye contact with all the interviewers. Breathe out, gently but purposefully.

Your turn

Be prepared for your turn – when you can ask the panel your questions. It's tactful to avoid questions about pay and holidays at this stage – all that can be discussed when an offer is made. So, focus on topics like training and development, opportunities to specialise, future plans for the organisation and the role. Try not to take too long – the candidate who gets out a list of questions fills the interview panel with dread. If you came prepared with questions, but in the course of your visit they have been answered, for example during a pre-interview talk or tour, then it's fine to say, 'Thank you, I did have some questions but they have all been covered.'

 **tip**

Being interviewed is a skill. As with any skill, you will get better with preparation, practice and feedback.

After the interview

If you are successful in your interview, your feedback will be that you are offered the job.

If you are not successful, you might want just to put it behind you and move on. However, if you do the two things we suggest here, your next interview will be better.

- **Firstly, reflect on your own performance**. While the interview is fresh in your mind, make a note of the questions you felt you struggled with, so that next time you can do a bit more preparation. Think too about the questions you felt you handled well and where the panel seemed to respond well – sounds like you have the right idea with those questions.

- **Secondly, seek feedback from the employer**. They are not obliged to give you feedback but, if you ask in the right way, i.e. that you want to learn from the experience for next time, not that you want to challenge the decision, then you may get something really useful. A helpful employer might say something like, 'In the interview, you didn't convince us that you would be an effective team member. You talked generally about teams you had been in without identifying your own role in the teams.' So make a list of the teams and groups you have been, or are, in and the role you play(ed). Next time around, then, you might be able to talk about your own part in a final-year group project – keeping the group to deadlines, or being the one with the creative ideas.

Even if you go for an interview, and you don't get it, you have moved forward because you'll learn from it. And if you get feedback, do listen to it.

Carl Gilleard, Chief Executive, Association of Graduate Recruiters

A word about telephone interviews

These are becoming increasingly common, especially as a first sift – they are a cheaper option for employers and candidates, but they present particular challenges. Almost everything we have already said applies, especially the importance of preparation. You might not need to put your interview suit on, but you really will perform better if you are in the right mind set, and being tidy and presentable is part of this. Sit at a desk or table (with paper and pen to hand) in a suitable environment, remove all background noise and make sure that there will be no interruptions. You will have no visual cues to help you and you need to concentrate even harder on what is being said and the impression that you are giving through your answers – pauses are particularly difficult on the phone compared with face to face. Don't be afraid to ask for a question to be repeated if you didn't hear it or if you are not clear what is meant.

brilliant example

'I applied online to a big company near Paris. I sent in my CV and a covering letter (in French). They did a telephone interview which was fact finding really. That was terrifying because I wasn't used to speaking French on the phone, but it went OK. They invited me to Paris for the second interview . . . there were the usual questions: strengths and weaknesses, experience of team work, that kind of thing. At the end of the interview she offered me a job on the spot.'

Hannah (Undergraduate), Economics and Politics with International Studies

Assessment centres

For our final section in this chapter, we'll take a look at assessment centres – what they are, how to prepare and how to find out more.

 **definition**

An **assessment centre** is a collection of activities that are designed to test candidates' suitability for a job.

Some of the activities are simulations of workplace tasks or activities, as many employers believe that such tasks give candidates a better chance to show their suitability for the job than a straightforward interview. They do not replace interviews though – typically an assessment centre might include short interviews, and then the most successful candidates are invited for a final, long interview.

Assessment centres can last for one day or more, and may even include cocktail parties and formal dinners.

There are usually several assessors, who may be assigned to individuals or to activities. The assessors will mark performance on each task according to predetermined scoring criteria. After all the tasks are completed and scored they will reach a collective view about candidates' suitability.

What they include

A typical assessment centre may include:

- **Psychometric tests**: as discussed earlier in this chapter.

- **Group discussions**: these could be on a work-related topic such as, 'How can this company increase its market share of 18–25 year olds?' Or a current affairs topic like, 'To what extent should economic migration to the UK be controlled?' The purpose is to assess candidates' ability to speak and listen, to persuade, to seek agreement, to contribute without dominating. If the topic is job-related, candidates' contributions could be assessed for the extent to which they demonstrate business awareness and understanding of the organisation.

- **Group tasks**: again, this might involve a job-related task, such as, 'Devise a marketing strategy to reach 18–25 year olds', or an apparently irrelevant task like contructing a bridge from Lego. Candidates are assessed for the extent to which they contribute to the successful completion of the task, and the role they play in the group.

- **Presentations**: these assess the ability to communicate in a clear, structured and persuasive manner. An additional challenge might be to prepare the presentation in a very short time, say 20 minutes.

- **Simulations**: these are tasks that resemble activities which occur in the job. A popular simulation is the 'in-tray exercise' where, candidates are asked to indicate how, and in what order, they would tackle a collection of messages and requests they might find on their desk on arrival at work.

- **Job-related tests**: these are activities that assess specific skills and knowledge required in the job and that candidates would have been expected to develop in their previous work or study. For example, preparing a budget based on information supplied, or demonstrating competence in specialist software.

- **Case studies and scenarios**: candidates, either individually or in groups, are presented with a job-related situation and asked to answer specific questions or to make recommendations on how the situation could be addressed.

- **Social events**: these can range from a 'cocktail party' setting to a formal dinner. Candidates are assessed for their ability to identify and interact with key people in the room, to engage in social interaction, and even for their table manners where formal dining might be part of the job role. Assessors are looking particularly for candidates' ability to remain professional in an apparently off-duty setting where there may be generous supplies of alcohol and food.

An employer with a group of applicants may programme the day as a 'carousel', so that, while some candidates are carrying out psychometric tests, others may be tackling a group task.

 **tip**

In an assessment centre, remember that you are under observation at all times, including meals and social time, so stay professional.

How to prepare

You may already be hoping that you will never be invited to an assessment centre – but it need not be daunting, especially if you think about two things:

- what the employer is looking for;
- what you have already done that will prepare you for the assessment centre.

You know what the employer is looking for from the person specification for the job – and by putting yourself in the employer's shoes. Good interpersonal skills, showing initiative without being pushy, the ability to complete a task accurately and under pressure, sensitivity to and awareness of others – these are all fairly obvious requirements of most jobs. However, remember that the employer is looking for evidence, and the assessment centre is an ideal source of first-hand evidence as it provides it in a number of ways.

In terms of what you have already done that will help to prepare you, look back at the list of likely activities we have just mentioned. You have a lot to draw on – presentations in seminars, group projects, organising your work as a deadline approaches – and we have already talked earlier in this chapter about preparation for psychometric tests.

So, to prepare for an assessment centre:

- think about what the employer wants;
- identify what you have already done that might make you feel more familiar with, and therefore less intimidated by, the tasks you are asked to do;

- check with your university careers service to see if they do practice assessment centres;

- use some of the excellent books on the subject – see our 'Further reading' section at the end of this book.

 **recap**

- To succeed in selection, make sure you know what the employer is looking for.

- Focus in particular on the person specification for the job.

- Employers use tests, interviews and assessment centres to select staff; make sure that you understand and are prepared for all these methods.

CHAPTER 12

My decision, my context, my life: why all this matters

This might seem like a very heavy title. Put more simply, the purpose of our final chapter is to help you to recognise and take into account the factors about you and your circumstances that may influence your career choices. Some circumstances might be outside your control, for example a shortage of jobs due to the economic climate but, even if you can't change these circumstances, you can adapt to them so that you gain in the longer term.

▶ brilliant example

'When I started at university I never thought for a second that I would be a teacher. It shows that what you learn along the way is so important to your ultimate career destination, and how much the path changes each day.'

Becky, BA (Hons) French and Tourism, now a primary school teacher

Decisions in context

Firstly, it's important to remember that none of us makes decisions in isolation. You might have a dream holiday destination – but the decision about where you actually go is influenced by cost, your availability, the availability of the holiday, your companions' wishes, and so on.

Who would you rather be?

Because you are positive and proactive, in planning your holiday you work with each of the factors we have just mentioned, deciding if you can do anything to give you more choice – do some extra hours at work to increase your budget, be more flexible with dates or destinations. Unless things go very wrong, you should still end up somewhere you want to be and be able to look back on an enjoyable experience.

Your friend, however, takes the passive, negative approach. She goes with the flow even if it's not what she wants, because she can't be bothered to get involved, or she opts out because her choice isn't on offer. She ends up spending the whole time resenting the fact that it isn't her choice, or worse, grumbling at home because she isn't going on holiday. Who would you rather be?

 **tip**

Don't opt out, opt in. Be positive and proactive in your approach to career decisions.

Factors that affect career decisions

If we extend the example of the holiday decision in the last section to career decisions, we can identify aspects of your personal circumstances and preferences that could be relevant to your choice of career. We can call these personal factors.

In Chapter 2 we talked about supply and demand in the graduate labour market; the demand for the kind of job you have in mind is very much influenced by external factors, which are outside your own control, but which have a key impact on your choices.

Here are some examples of these two kinds of factors, and how they might impact on your career plans.

Personal factors and their impact on career plans

- **Family circumstances**: is anyone relying on your income? Are you a carer for a child, a younger sibling, a sick or elderly relative? Do you have a partner who is committed to a course or job in a particular area? *Impact*: you may need to look for work in a particular location; your available hours for work may be determined by your responsibilities for others; you may feel under pressure to take any job in order to bring money in; or you may have to delay your entry to the labour market.

- **Finances**: apart from repaying your student loan (which applies to most graduates) do you have any significant debts? Do you have savings, or access to financial support? *Impact*: you may feel that you have to take any job to start to pay off debt; alternatively, if you have savings and/or financial support, this could give you freedom to undertake further study or voluntary work.

- **Location**: do you need to stay in or return to a particular area, for example because of family circumstances? Do you have preferences about location and how important are they? Are you willing to move for work? Can you drive? *Impact*: opportunities may be more limited if your location is restricted, and conversely more wide ranging if you are willing to move. Housing/living costs in a new location may be relevant.

- **Family influence**: is there an expectation that you will enter an occupation held by your parents, or that you will join a family business? Will your choice of career be a family decision, or one made by you alone? *Impact*: it could be helpful to enter an occupation that you know intimately, including understanding the benefits and drawbacks for your way of life. A family business might provide a good start, especially if opportunities are otherwise limited. In either case you can work towards a specialist area based on your interests and preferences.

- **Further study and training**: are you willing and able to commit to further study? If full-time, how will you support yourself financially? *Impact*: some jobs require further study so, if this really isn't an option, you may have to re-plan or defer entry.

- **An existing job**: could you work full-time for the employer you have worked for during university? Are you under pressure from the employer to do so? What's in it for you if you do?
  Impact: this route could leave you wondering why you went to university; alternatively, it could give you the prospect of a graduate-level job by another route.

- **A grand plan**: do you have a longer-term aim that is influencing what you do after university?
  Impact: sticking rigidly to a set plan can be dangerous if it just leaves you marking time; it can be good if you use the time constructively.

- **Health**: is there anything about your health that might have implications for your choice of job?
  Impact: there may be some jobs from which you are excluded (e.g. people with epilepsy cannot usually work with machinery), or some that you need to seek out, for example a job where you are mainly sitting down. Be aware that, if you have a disability, you have certain entitlements by law; if you meet the selection criteria for a job you must be offered an interview; and once you are in employment, your employer is expected to make reasonable adjustments to your workplace and equipment to enable you to carry out your work.

Reasons, not excuses

brilliant definitions

A **reason** is an attempt to explain.

An **excuse** is an attempt to avoid.

It might help to assess where you stand in respect of each of these personal factors, both now and in the future, and to consider what is negotiable and what isn't. You might not like working at weekends because it interferes with your social life, but is it a reason? On the other hand, you might coach a junior football team on Sundays and just now there isn't anyone else, it's a tough part of town, and you won't let them down.

Once you have identified honestly what is non-negotiable, be positive, not apologetic, both with employers and with yourself – it's a reason, not an excuse; and review regularly – circumstances change, a new coach comes along, your partner finishes their course so you can relocate – and you can reassess your situation.

 **tip**

Review your personal circumstances regularly – a change of situation may enable you to broaden your job search.

External factors

There is really just one, big external factor affecting graduate jobs and that is the economic climate. More localised events that impact on jobs, such as the opening or closing of finance houses, production plants and distribution centres, are all the result of changes in the economic landscape. We cannot pretend that there is no impact, because there is. However, what we can do is to encourage you to look behind the scaremongering headlines. A year or two ago, at the start of the recession, graduate unemployment had its biggest increase for some years, up from 5.5 per cent to 7.9 per cent. This was presented in some parts of the media as a 45 per cent increase in graduate unemployment. While this is accurate when the increase of 2.4 per cent is taken as a percentage of the previous year's figure of 5.5 per cent, it looked at first sight very alarming and disguised the fact that 92.1 per cent of graduates did enter jobs or further study. So do get accurate data, especially about your own subject area and your own university. Have another look at Chapter 3 for an analysis of what graduates do, and talk to your university careers service for information about recent graduates from your university.

'Within two months of leaving university, in a very tough economic climate, I had secured a great job, providing consultancy to some large firms. I had delivered workshops, presentations and pitches to both sole traders and national companies. I believe my time at university equipped me with the creative problem-solving skills and self-awareness I needed to excel within my industry.'

Alex, BA (Hons) Graphic Design

Experts predict that the economy will recover and, when it does, there will be even more need for well-qualified entrants to the labour market. In the meantime, what this means for you is that:

- it may take longer to get to where you want to be;
- you might go by an unexpected route.

If you do find yourself in the very unfortunate position of not having a job, not having anything to do and there's nothing in the pipeline, you must do something to get yourself out of that rut. Any job is better than no job. If it's not a job, if it's voluntary work or a training course . . . there's a whole range of things you could be doing.

Carl Gilleard, Chief Executive, Association of Graduate Recruiters

If at first you don't succeed

Mind your language

If you have identified factors in your own context that will influence your career planning, then you need to work with these factors, rather than regarding them as barriers to a graduate job. Even small statements can signal this kind of positive approach. Compare these two:

> I can't drive so I'm limited to jobs in this town.

or

> I'm looking for work that is accessible by public transport and I'm willing to travel for up to 90 minutes each way.

The first contains two negatives – 'can't' and 'limited'; the second, two active positives – 'looking' and 'willing'.

Now these two:

> I can't work in school holidays because of my children, so I probably won't be able to get a job until they are old enough to leave.

or

> I'm exploring all the organisations that might offer term-time-only work – not just schools, but colleges, the local university, and the local authority Children's Services Department. My friend works in Governor Services and has a really interesting job supporting school governing bodies – and it's term-time only.'

Again we can see 'can't' and 'won't', compared with 'exploring'.

There is very clear evidence from psychological research, which shows us that a change in attitude can lead to a change in behaviour. So look again at the second example in each pair. The positive statements are a clear indication of jobsearch behaviour. So, if you can adopt a more positive attitude, this will have an impact on your behaviour.

Can you turn the following statements round to demonstrate a more positive approach?

- 'I want to keep on living here after university because all my house-mates are staying, but I don't know if there are any jobs.'

- 'I might as well stay on at the supermarket after I graduate – they've offered me a job and the papers say there aren't any graduate jobs.'

- 'I need to clear my debts so I have so stay on in the bar where I've been working.'

- 'There's no point in doing any voluntary work because I'd only have to give it up if I get a job.'

- 'No one from this university ever gets into a blue chip company so there's no point in applying.'

- 'If only I had a 2:1 instead of a 2:2, it would make all the difference.'

- 'Yes, but what about all the other people who'll apply for that job?'

So, reflect on the language you use – not just in applications and careers interviews, but in informal conversations with your family and friends and, if you hear lots of negatives, try to turn your language around to signal a positive, constructive approach.

You've got to remain positive. I'll give you one guarantee: if you give up, you'll never get a job. And it's easier to get a job when you're in employment than when you're unemployed. Any job is better than no job. That's the starting point.

Carl Gilleard, Chief Executive, Association of Graduate Recruiters

Enhance your skills and learning

Increasing the range of opportunities open to you calls for creative approaches. The best counterbalance to an unfulfilling job is to get involved in learning something new. Not only will you maintain the momentum of study you built up during your degree, but you will send a good signal about yourself to prospective employers – and you will ward off boredom. Here are some of the ways you can continue to study:

- Do a short course at your local further education or community college – IT, a language, or a project management course could all be useful in a future job. Get a prospectus online or enquire at your local library.

- Look at postgraduate study. If you can't afford to do a full-time course, you can study part-time or through distance or blended learning – we looked at these in detail in Chapter 6. Many universities offer single modules if you don't want to commit to a complete course.

- Maximise your chances of learning from your job. Look at training offered in the workplace – first aid, supervisory skills – or create your own learning – ask if you can assist with a special project or promotion. Look at this brilliant example.

▶ brilliant example

'One night the barman seemed to be on holiday, so they put me behind the bar on a busy night. I had done the dispensing bar, which was pretty straightforward, so when it was quiet I asked the bar supervisor to show me the cocktails. But it was like – what the hell am I doing? How can they expect me to do this when I've never done it in my life? I looked like a complete muppet . . . but I'll give anything a go once, and they figured out I could do it and I wasn't that bad, so they put me on the bar a lot more. And it's good because I can show that I've got more all-round experience and I'm happy to learn, and I'm flexible, so I will be able to negotiate a higher rate of pay when I go back next time.'

Hannah (Undergraduate), Economics and Politics with International Studies

- Create a portfolio of experience. For example, a psychology graduate interested in working in an advisory role with young people could take a counselling skills course in the evenings, do some voluntary work in an advice centre and support himself with a part-time job in retail or hospitality, both of which are excellent settings for developing skills with people. This three-part package will be far more use in developing his employment prospects than the job on its own.

Be in charge of yourself

In Chapter 1 we introduced you to the job fairy. It will sometimes seem as if other people get the benefit of this friendly little person, while you miss out; and it's certainly the case that some jobs come out of happy accidents and chance meetings. However, it's also the case that the people this happens to have their ears and eyes open, and respond positively to the opportunity presenting itself. So it's not entirely accidental after all. By all means get help from others – but recognise that you have the control, and no one else. You might have other people to think about, and other people's expertise to draw on, but you are still the person in charge of your future.

 **brilliant** tip

When it comes to your career plan, you are responsible for yourself and nobody else; and nobody else is responsible for you.

Moving on

Your second graduate job

This might seem an odd topic to introduce when you are probably still looking for your first one, but by the time this happens to you – two, three or four years down the line – you may feel cut adrift from the sources of help you have been able to use at university, so here are some thoughts for you to keep in the back of your mind till you need them.

brilliant dos and don'ts

Do

✔ use the skills of reflection we discussed in Chapter 7 to assess how your first job is going;

✔ record your key achievements along the way – they will be invaluable in updating your CV and in completing future applications;

✔ seek out professional help – some university careers services will help graduates with subsequent job moves for a fixed period of time after graduation. Others offer a fee-charging service to graduates from any university.

Don't

✘ move without giving your first job a chance. Discuss with your manager what you need to develop your experience and interest, and how your job will develop in the future, before you decide to move on.

In this example, Victoria, whom you met in Chapter 4, describes moving from her second to her third graduate job, so she is at a point of leverage rather than a point of entry.

brilliant example

'(In my second consultancy) I worked hard to get integrated and continue to pursue retail projects. However, I didn't feel there was much retail opportunity available so, after a year, I decided to leave and then find a new job. It's really hard to find a new job when you are working long days at your existing one!

I put my CV on Internet job boards and used my network of contacts from the two previous companies to find introductions at retail companies and also recruitment agencies.

I began by considering any job opportunity both consulting and "industry" (i.e. for actual retailers) but, as my search progressed, I realised I actually only wanted to work in "industry". I ended up with three offers on the table.'

Victoria, MA Geography

Notice that she was in a much stronger position than when she had first graduated, because she had her own network of contacts. Note too that the actual process of jobsearch helped her to identify her preferred focus.

Your life and why all this matters

As a current graduate, you will be affected by two of the biggest changes to working life in recent years.

Firstly, you will be working for longer than your parents did (but you will benefit from flexible working patterns, including homeworking).

Secondly, you will probably have several jobs and many careers during this time. It helps that relationships between health and well-being and job satisfaction are well established, and there is much more recognition of the need for a good balance between working life and life outside work. Some organisations even make provision for staff to have 'career breaks' of a few months' unpaid leave, to go on that trip of a lifetime.

So it's worth investing some time and effort on your career plan, not just now, but at key decision points as they come up. For example, it's never too late to start postgraduate study, and it's often even more rewarding and interesting when you have some experience behind you.

It's impossible to predict now what your working life will look like over the next 40 or so years. It will help if you are open to changes of direction and new opportunities and it's important to recognise that your own interests, skills and values will change over time and that good career progression need not necessarily be upwards.

 Most of those who are graduating now will have two or three careers – not jobs, careers. Be confident enough to step off the career ladder in order to be the best at what you do.

Carl Gilleard, Chief Executive, Association of Graduate Recruiters

We wish you the very best of luck for your future and we hope that our book is there for you along the way – and remember, you are the one in control of your brilliant graduate career.

Online resources

www.careersbox.co.uk

A site that shows films of real people talking from their workplaces about the jobs they do in a wide range of occupational sectors.

www.eu-student.eu

Comprehensive guide to the Erasmus programme for study and internships within EU (internships minimum one month).

www.fco.gov.uk/en/travel-and-living-abroad

For travel advice by country.

www.flyingstartonline.com

Linked to the National Council for Graduate Entrepreneurship, this website is dedicated to getting student and graduate business started.

www.graduatetalentpool.direct.gov.uk

Information about, and details of, internships.

www.gradunet.com

Web-based job listing for graduates.

www.gttr.ac.uk

The Graduate Teacher Training Registry: official website where you can research postgraduate programmes and apply online.

www.hesa.ac.uk

Higher Education Statistics Agency: range of publications including *Destinations of Leavers from Higher Education* (*DLHE*).

www.jobcentreonline.com

Vacancies notified to the Northern Ireland job services, so restricted to that geographical area.

www.jobs.nhs.uk

Comprehensive guide to all NHS vacancies. This includes healthcare professions, but also a range of technical and management jobs.

www.jobseekers.direct.gov.uk

Official government jobs site: vacancies searchable by region, industry or company.

www.mastersportal.eu

Lists postgraduate programmes across the EU, covers Masters and doctoral level; useful search engine.

www.milkround.com

A member of the News International Group, this website lists graduate jobs and internships.

www.monster.co.uk

Online job vacancy site, searchable by occupational or geographical area; useful company profile feature.

www.ncge.com

National Council for Graduate Entrepreneurship: lots of advice for graduates who are interested in self-employment as an option.

www.prospects.ac.uk

Comprehensive online information, advice and guidance for students in higher education.

www.roberthalf.co.uk

UK-wide vacancies in the financial services sector. This includes accounting, finance and related management, extending to specialist technical services.

www.statistics.gov.uk

Office for National Statistics (ONS) publishes official statistics for the United Kingdom, including reports on the labour market in general.

www.thegraduate.co.uk

Web-based job listing for graduates; includes placement, undergraduate and postgraduate-level opportunities.

www.ukces.org.uk

UK Commission for Employment and Skills: up-to-date articles on skills demand and sector changes.

Further reading

Ashley, R. (2006) *Improving your Employability*. London: Teach Yourself.

BIS (2010). *Small and Medium-sized Enterprise (SME) Statistics for the UK and Regions 2009 (SME Statistics)*. London: Department for Business, Innovation and Skills (BIS).

Bright, J. and Earl, J. (2011) *Brilliant CV: What employers want to see and how to write it*. 4th edn. Harlow: Prentice Hall.

Byron, M. (2010) *The Graduate Psychometric Test Workbook*. London: Kogan Page.

Carter, P.J. (2007) *IQ and Personality Tests*. London: Kogan Page.

CBI (2009a) *Future fit: preparing graduates for the world of work*. Confederation of British Industry. London: CBI.

CBI (2009b) *Stronger Together: Businesses and universities in turbulent times*. Available online **http://highereducation.cbi.org.uk/uploaded/CBI_HE_taskforce_report.pdf.**

CIHE (2008) *Graduate Employability: What do employers think and want?* London: Council for Industry and Higher Education.

Hind, D. and Moss, S. (2007) *Employability Skills*. Sunderland: Business Education Publishers.

Hodgson, S. (2005) *Brilliant Answers to Tough Interview Questions*. 2nd edn. Harlow: Prentice Hall.

Hodgson, S. (2008) *Brilliant Tactics to Pass Aptitude Tests*. 2nd edn. Harlow: Prentice Hall.

Parkinson, M. (2008) *How to Master Psychometric Tests*. London: Kogan Page.

Taylor, D. (2010) *Now You've Been Shortlisted*. Petersfield: Harriman.